CUTTINGS

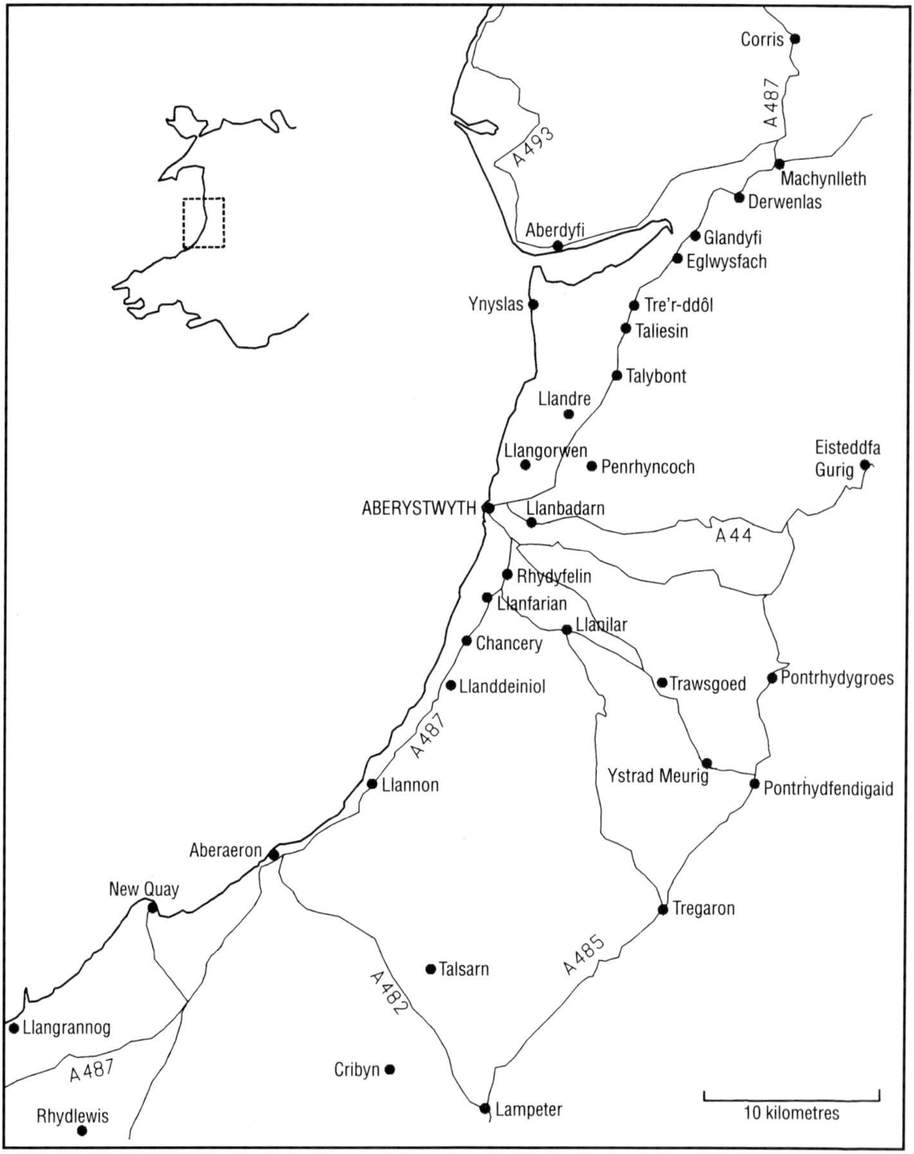

Corris
A 487
A 493
Machynlleth
Derwenlas
Aberdyfi
Glandyfi
Eglwysfach
Ynyslas
Tre'r-ddôl
Taliesin
Talybont
Llandre
Llangorwen
Penrhyncoch
Eisteddfa Gurig
ABERYSTWYTH
Llanbadarn
A 44
Rhydyfelin
Llanfarian
Llanilar
Chancery
Trawsgoed
Pontrhydygroes
Llanddeiniol
A 487
Ystrad Meurig
Llannon
Pontrhydfendigaid
Aberaeron
New Quay
Tregaron
A 485
Talsarn
A 482
Llangrannog
A 487
Cribyn
Lampeter
10 kilometres
Rhydlewis

Cuttings

A Gardeners' pot pourri from Wales

Caroline Palmer

Illustrations by Jenny Fell

GOMER

First Publication—November 1996

ISBN 0 185902 402 5

Printed in Wales at
Gomer Press, Llandysul, Ceredigion

To the many readers of my column,
who gave me the encouragement and confidence to continue,
and to my family,
who sometimes allowed me a modicum of peace.

Contents

january

A bouquet for New Year's Day

Speaking on Radio 4 recently, David Wheeler, editor of *Hortus*, urged us all to go outdoors on New Year's Day and record the number of species in bloom in the garden.

'That won't take long' was my initial reaction, remembering only snowdrops and the winter jasmine, loyally yellow-starred on the front wall of the house. However, my circuit of the garden yielded a respectable little posy in white, purple and yellow. I found the Spanish broom, *Genista hispanica*, speckled with tiny yellow flowers—smaller perhaps than its summer blooms, but as brilliant as the gorse flowers on the hillside above—and the first contorted strips of lemon-peel flowers on my young witch hazel. On the sheltered side of the shrubby laurustinus were large flat heads of the small fleshy white flowers. Three different species of hellebore were in bloom too, green cascades of flowers on the *Helleborus foetidus*, and an early spray on *Helleborus argutifolius*. Thoroughly ahead of itself, in view of its common English name, was the Lenten rose, *Helleborus orientalis*, each nodding white bud already opening to form a bell. Those other green-flowered treasures, the spurges, already showed conspicuous buds, but perhaps could not quite qualify as blooms.

The winter heather, *Erica carnea*, properly flowers from December, and 'Springwood White' rewarded my eye with a snowy mass of tiny flowers each flushed with pink and exquisitely tipped in deep burgundy. The perennial wallflower *Erysimum* 'Bowles' Mauve' boasted several handsome spikes of purple flowers above its silver-grey leaves. My Universal Series pansies, almost all purple ones this year, fulfilled their promise with abundant flowers, and near the bird bath I found its little self-seeded relative, *Viola tricolor*, the heartsease, in equally enthusiatic bloom.

Thus inspired, I visited Llidiardau, a friend's garden farther up the Ystwyth Valley, a few days later. Here the first white buds were breaking open on the finely scented *Viburnum* x *burkwoodii*, and the leafless *Viburnum* x *bodnantense* was decked with pink clusters of flowers. We found salmon-pink flowers on the Japanese quince, and in full flower, the fragrant *Sarcococca hookeriana* in which the tiny pinkish flowers hang in ragged clusters from beneath the leaf axils.

Just peeping above the leafmould, we dicovered the tiny strong pink *Cyclamen coum* and a few early primroses. In squelchy ground at the streamside we found the first blooms of the winter heliotrope, *Petasites fragrans*, a European wildflower now naturalized in gardens. With the newly emerging coltsfoot-like leaves comes a cluster of pale lilac flowers on a stout bract-covered stem. Stooping, one is rewarded by a pungent scent of vanilla.

The kitchen garden yielded sweet rocket and broccoli in bloom. We also found two weeds in flower, Buxbaum's speedwell, *Veronica persica*, and the dreaded rosettes of jumping Jesus, or hairy bittercress. Little wonder these two weeds are well ahead of me by the time spring is here.

1995

Mistletoe seeds in apple trees

Possibly worth salvaging from the wreckage of Christmas adornments is the mistletoe, for I would welcome a handsome green orb of mistletoe among the branches of my apple trees. Some years ago there was a fine plant in a tree near the bottom of Penglais Hill, Aberystwyth but one day the tree was chopped down and now I know of no good-sized plants this side of Herefordshire.

Ideally the berries should be stored in moist sand until late February or March, for, as with most plants, early germination followed by a severe cold snap can be disastrous. Most experts then recommend the seeds should be planted by making a cross-shaped incision in the bark of the tree, preferably on the under surface, and then poking in the single seed from within the fleshy white berry. The naturally sticky viscin, which surrounds the seed, holds it firmly in place. The individual seeds are pointed at one end like an apple pip, and it is the pointed end from which the radicle or future root appears.

As long ago as the nineteenth century French naturalists recorded that unlike most seeds, from which the root responds to gravity and grows downwards, the radicle of the mistletoe defies gravity and always points towards the centre of the host branch to which it is attached.

In a year or two, successful germination should lead to the appearance of a small green disc on the branch surface, and from this the first bifurcated green twig of mistletoe.

My own efforts have as yet come to naught but I was delighted to learn from Arthur Newman of Capel Dewi that he has recently found a young mistletoe plant sprouting on the apple tree where two years ago his wife inserted the seeds. For saleable fruiting sprigs he will need at least two such plants, for mistletoe is single-sexed, and male and female plants are needed. Tiny pale yellowy green flowers appear in groups of three at the forks of the green stems in early spring, and on the female plants will swell to the familiar dull white winter berries. However, it is a slow crop, taking up to seven years to reach fruiting size.

Much commercially available mistletoe is imported for the Christmas trade from Normandy, where huge orbs of mistletoe in the poplars adjoining the roads and railway lines are even more conspicuous than the apple orchard plants. British mistletoe comes chiefly from the orchards of Hereford and the West Country.

Although all European mistletoe is a single species, *Viscum album*, it is said that seeds prefer to grow upon the same kind of tree as that on which the parent plant was attached. It may thus be less auspicious to plant French poplar mistletoe on one's apple tree. On the other hand I doubt if the mistle thrushes, which are credited as the chief planters of mistletoe, are that particular where they clean their beaks, so, notwithstanding my ignorance of its provenance, I shall go ahead and try to plant the seeds of our seasonal sprig in the upper branches of my Bramley apple trees.

1992

On the habits of hedgehogs

My family Christmas has been dominated by a hedgehog—not one of those lumbering, snuffling flea-transporters now cosily tucked up in the bottom of the pile of hedge trimmings, but a blue spiky hedgehog of extraordinary athletic prowess, a hedgehog with a partiality for gold rings, daring leaps and for destroying enemies by jumping upon their heads.

I am not certain whether the Japanese people have a hedgehog on their islands, but even if they do, this hedgehog, brainchild of the team of creative artists who design Sega computer games, would be equally outlandish in that ecology. It may, none the less, prove a worthy recipient of the title 'Gardener's Friend', for there seems little doubt that Sonic the Hedgehog, battling against a robotic enemy and, incidentally, releasing furry friends like rabbits and squirrels as he triumphs, has greatly reduced child-induced wear on my garden over the holiday period.

In the cold sunshine of the Christmas break, the real rabbits and squirrels were unusually frequent visitors to the garden, drawn by the hard weather to exhibit their more unlovable habits of grazing upon the bark of winter trees. The last rows of carrots have also suffered, their crowns of leaves nibbled, or indeed the whole top of the root gnawed out to below ground level.

The squirrels and rabbits are usually deterred by our cat, which thankfully much prefers red meat to bird and demonstrates his prowess by leaving large squashy entrails and soft floppy rabbit ears on the apple-loft floor. However, with the winter chill it seems he felt himself better employed by the fireside, and it was a common sight to see his prey lolloping across the grass or pausing to chew on a windfall apple.

Real hedgehogs, like the cat, are concentrating on their slumber at this time of year, and hibernate so deeply that it is important to turn and rebuild a bonfire pile thoroughly before setting it alight on a crisp January day. Quite apart from their natural charm, real hedgehogs are a garden asset when awake and on the prowl (not normally until around mid-March). They will root out a prodigious number of caterpillars, beetles, earthworms, slugs, snails and leather-jackets. Despite their unstreamlined shape, they are quite effective climbers, and will scale walls and trees in search of slugs and snails. In addition to their obvious protective function, the spikes on a hedgehog are an excellent shock-absorber. Climbing hedgehogs suddenly dislodged may not land cat-like upon their paws, but they do bounce.

There are some well-worn jokes about the hedgehog's spines and how, with such exteriors, hedgehogs achieve hedgehog intimacy. Along a similar train of thought it is a comfort to know that new-born baby hedgehogs are smooth and naked, the spines emerging a few hours after birth. One would imagine that natural selection deals summarily and harshly with an overdue hedgehog baby.

1993

Building a garden pool

It was at about this time last year that my ornamental pond began to take shape, initially as an irregular hole gouged in a few deft bucket loads of a JCB from the wreckage of my lawn after the completion of our extension. The books do assert that January or February is the ideal time for the commencement of a pond and my subsequent experience has confirmed this. The small stone-edged pool, margined with seared *Miscanthus* grasses sheltering a pocket of bog garden, already looks as if it had been there for ever. It is just a short distance outside the window, and because the land slopes up from the house, the water surface is more or less on a level with the windowsill. This has visual benefits which I did not foresee when I designed it. On bright days, sunlight is reflected upwards on to the ceiling where it shimmers and wavers in the new room. With an overcast sky and a westerly wind the water is thrown into lapping iron-grey ripples. Today the picture is different again, with the frozen water surface drawn into a random arrangement of nine-inch-long, horizontal intermeshing icicles, and little petrified ripples at the windy side. The cold water beneath the ice is motionless and clear, the five goldfish hanging like lamps beneath its surface.

In building the pond, I enlisted the help of local gardener and pond enthusiast Ian Finlay, for it is clearly a job in which there is no substitute for practical experience. If there is one aspect which merits obsessive care it is the adjustment of the levels of the pond margins before the liner is installed. Nothing is a harsher judge of a level surface than a sheet of water and too many hastily constructed ponds suffer from that amateurish look where the pond liner is on permanent view above the water level at one side of the pond. Exposed directly to air and sunlight, this unsightly margin also decays sooner and hastens the end of the pond. Ian spent a long time with shovel, trowel and a spirit level balanced upon a plank ensuring that the future pond was set absolutely level into the sloping terrain in which it lay. The stone margin which secures the pond liner would thus overlap the water on the downside, but form a retaining wall with a broad flat top holding back the rising ground above the pond.

The hole meanwhile partially filled up with rather foul-smelling seepage from the hillside (our septic tank was not far away) which would prevent the rubber liner snugly fitting the hole. It took us many failed attempts before we set up a siphon to draw away the water: all too often the hose would suck up mud and pebbles and block itself before the level had dropped. At last it was achieved, and in the teeth of a rain squall we unfolded the heavy rubber liner and clambered gingerly about on its surface arranging the heavy folds as we filled up the lined pond with clean water. It was just when I was knee-deep and mud-covered that a sales assistant from Austin Reed telephoned to demand some trivial detail about my husband's credit card!

It was all straightforward from then on. Over a number of days Ian built the stone margin, using large flat walling stones and some extra-big river boulders to frame the neck between open water and the rubber-lined, earth-filled bog garden. Where the level of the margin necessarily changed we used a substantial step rather than a slope to join the levels and these make appealing perches on which to sit and gaze into the pond.

I began to plant the pond in April, using submersible plastic basins for the small water lilies *Nymphaea* x *marliacea* and black baskets for the marginal water plants submerged at the shallow edges. By summer, with mating pairs of red damsel flies dancing over the surface, coupled together like twin-rotor helicopters, and the population of water skaters ranging from adult to the tiniest of high-speed specks, there was plenty to gaze upon. There's always something going on in a pond, and even my six-year-old and her friend would often choose to take out toys, or a sewing game, and play quietly at its edge.

1995

Scented flowers for the *cognoscenti*

Pleasure is perhaps most keenly felt when reality exceeds expectation. To see snowdrops may be expected, to find them carpeting an untrodden acre of woodland is a thrill. No less so was my delight at finding, this week, a flower on my wintersweet, and when I say flower in the singular, I mean it, for my bush has rewarded me for years of patience with just one individual bloom. An added dimension to my delight is that it occurred to me to go out and look at the shrub; how easily it could have had its first record-breaking flower unobserved.

Wintersweet (*Chimonanthus praecox*) is one of the choice elements in the winter garden, highly prized by the likes of Vita Sackville-West and Margery Fish, gardeners with plenty of time and space at their disposal. It is less frequently extolled for smaller modern gardens, where instant results are often expected and a shrub is expected to pay its way all the year round. Wintersweet does neither of these things. It covers itself in summer with entirely ordinary-looking, slightly serrated green leaves, which drop off without any undue display of autumn colour, and are replaced in succeeding years by similar foliage. If it does not flower, it does nothing of note. Textbook illustrations show the twigs lined with flowers, each downward-pointing, many-petalled and a straw yellow in colour. Closer inspection of my solitary bloom shows inner petals mottled with dark red. But it is for its scent that the wintersweet is justly celebrated. It is difficult to describe scent, but terms borrowed from the wine-taster like rich and full-bodied spring to mind. It is said that a single flowering twig will scent a room. Perhaps next year I shall be in a position to test it.

Another winter-scented flower for the *cognoscenti* is *Lonicera* x *purpusii*, which flourishes in Halcyon Hinde's garden on The Buarth, Aberystwyth. Her January bouquet of garden flowers at the recent Cardiganshire Horticultural Society meeting included this white-flowering Chinese honeysuckle, its leafless twigs abundantly flowered, and sweetly fragrant. As Halcyon remarked, it is hardly worth the space it occupies for the rest of the year, forming an untidy mounded bush, largely leafless in winter, about five foot high.

More of an all-round performer for the small garden is *Daphne odora*, a spruce little bush with glossy evergreen leaves and waxy pink and white flowers. It takes a long time to become large but will come home flowering obligingly in its garden-centre container. It is also excellent for scent. Others will favour the earliest of the viburnums, *Viburnum* x *bodnantense*, which clusters its pale pink flowers in knots along the bare twigs. Both flowers and leaves of this shrub are scented, but the scent is not as exquisite as that of either honeysuckle or wintersweet.

I must admit to an irrational dislike of mahonias, which always strike me as a perfectly adequate but inelegant plant. But were I to grow a mahonia, it would not be 'Charity', the best seller of the cultivars, but the plain species *Mahonia japonica*. This has spreading sprays of yellow flowers arising from the tip of each shoot, and by far the strongest and most pleasing scent.

1995

Some cheerful survivors of a squelchy winter

I have barely ventured into the garden in the last month, driven indoors by the seemingly endless succession of depressions bringing wind and rain. However, with the recent bright cold spell came a renewed optimism and the urge to assess the winter's progress.

The primrose bank is sadly depleted this year. Sometimes I have had a pleasing show by Christmas, but this year only a few apologetic blooms are to be seen, plastered down on earth smoothed and waterlogged by successive deluges.

Slugs have almost entirely consumed the mat of burgundy-hued bugle, *Ajuga reptans,* at the bank foot; the leafless stems bearing tattered clusters of tiny leaves snake across the bare earth. Only the *Lobelia cardinalis* pushing up fresh red-hued rosettes and the mats of mossy saxifrage look spruce and undamaged.

In the orchard, where since autumn the gentle slope has been carpeted with small windfalls, hazardous as ball bearings underfoot, the going is now easier. In the last weeks hordes of squabbling starlings have abandoned their probings in the pastures in favour of my apples, and have joined the large number of resident blackbirds which hop constantly among the fruit. Now there are only hollow beak-pecked apple skins, a little slippy and slimy underfoot but likely to be almost gone by the time snowdrops and aconites are out.

At this time of year one is particularly grateful to those few substantial herbaceous plants which retain some winter integrity in the blasted borders. Foremost in my esteem are the green-flowered hellebores and certain euphorbias whose strongly sculptural evergreen leaves give comfort to the eye. *Euphorbia robbiae*, hardy, leathery relative of the tender and exotic Christmas poinsettia, displays bushy clumps of dark green rosettes without blemish even after the punishing conditions of the past month. This is a spurge so unfashionable that it is rarely mentioned in plant books and almost never illustrated. Beth Chatto is, I believe, its only champion amongst present gardening writers. It is a vigorous plant, familiar in older gardens, which forms attractive year-round clumps in awkward dry shade beneath trees and will flourish in the ordinary border. It flowers in early summer, a luminous broad head of greenish-yellow spurge flowers which remain for several months. Some may find it too invasive, for it spreads by underground runners, but these incursions are easily halted by an annual chop with the spade.

1991

Seeds or plantlets for the coming year

Perhaps my greatest gardening disappointment of last season was my packet of Dobies' poppies, 'Summer Breeze F_1'. These looked charming in the illustration: compact grey-green finely cut foliage in neat clumps, each topped by a mass of handsome wide-eyed poppy flowers in orange, clear yellow, or luminous white with a golden eye. In my mind's eye I saw them, massed as poppies should be, twelve to fourteen inches tall to the front of the border.

Opening the tiny foil-lined packet I felt a certain dismay. Poppy seeds are about the size of a grain of salt. In the whole of the packet there were just twenty of these tiny specks of dust. This was foreseeable, for seeds bearing the suffix F_1 are the product of controlled pollination of one plant by another, usually dissimilar, parent. F_1 seeds are therefore time-consuming to produce and cannot be harvested from a field-grown row of the plants; they are relatively expensive and sold in smaller numbers than the hundreds one might expect in a packet of foxgloves or lobelias.

Hardly daring to breathe, I sprinkled my twenty seeds on the seed compost and sieved a little fine compost over them. I tended them in a propagator and soon they germinated—tiny, fragile, hairlike plants bearing their first two leaves. Then they began to sulk. They grew very little except to elongate and drape their translucent stems across the surface. Some then damped off. It was weeks before the others were large enough to be cautiously transplanted into individual pots. Not till late August did I see my first flower. My eventual yield was just five plants, all irritatingly identical orange-hued, all undersized, and all too late.

No doubt my lack of expertise was to blame, but in this I am not alone. It is experiences like this which fuel the market for healthy young plantlets, and the seed merchants are rapidly expanding this side of their business. Most now sell a limited range of tiny well-rooted plants; Dobies call them Easiplants, Thompson and Morgan call them Speedplugs, Marshalls call them Starterplants. They come in an expanded polystyrene tray of some thirty-five small, highly fertile compost plugs, and unless seriously delayed should arrive in good condition. (If they don't, complain: reputable plant companies replace or refund damaged or delayed plants without question.) This is quite a costly way of gardening, since thirty-five plants cost, depending on variety, between £7 and £9, but results are almost guaranteed. Plants are propagated to order, so most companies specify a last order date in February for any of these lines. Delivery will be in April, so it could be important to foresee holiday absences and to ensure sufficient windowsill and greenhouse space to grow on the new purchases until frosts are past.

Certain stalwart seeds I shall continue to buy: *Cosmos* 'Sonata White' for its hovering white flowers and ferny foliage; clary, the romantic *Salvia horminium,* whose mass of pink, white and purple-bracted stems form a haze of colour around my bird bath, and the glossy cerise-flowered flax *Linum grandiflorum rubrum* which, scattered freely, will spring up among rocks and low-growing plants. But perhaps I shall leave other tasks for the specialists, buying godetias, snapdragons and lavatera as locally grown strips, and even splashing out £7.25 on some well brought up 'Summer Breeze' poppies.

1994

february

furnace. The chimney from this furnace runs, as a salt-glazed clay pipe, horizontally beneath two richly loamy beds before venting at the surface. Gently heated by the warm air from beneath and protected by glass frames above, it is little wonder that Llanerchaeron in the nineteenth century could supply melons and pineapples to all the surrounding gentry.

Llanerchaeron has been empty since it was left to the National Trust five years ago, and negotiations about ownership and long-term funding have been prolonged and complex. Restoration work is now getting under way upon the outbuildings. When I visited, two masons were tidily replacing the coping bricks on the wall of the farther walled garden. Soon the house itself will disappear from view, wrapped in a sheath of rainproof material while coats of limewash are applied. This season only the grounds will be open to the public. Were it not for the activities of the Llanerchaeron volunteer gardeners there would be precious little but rampant undergrowth for them to admire.

1995

Victims of the storm of 1990

Spared, as we were, the full force of the 1987 hurricane, most of us were taken by surprise by the gale of January 25, 1990, which made an unprecedented challenge upon trees and glasshouses alike. Almost everybody has some damage to report and even in gardens devoid of large and vulnerable plants, the dehydrating damage of windburn upon normally resilient leaves like those of privet is quite noticeable.

However, it was the older houses of substance whose gardens tended to fare worst in the gale. At Cwmcynfelin near Aberystwyth, the handsome old cedar of Lebanon in the parkland facing the house lost a great branch torn from the crown. Beyond it three large specimen silver birches were tipped over in the wind, while in the sheltering plantation which borders the driveway the wind cut a swathe through the spruces, toppling them till their flat root bases stood on edge. It was a matter of both relief and surprise that the great wellingtonia

(*Sequoiadendron giganteum*) flexed dramatically in the wind but sustained no damage.

At Brongennau Hall, Llandre, the devastation was even greater. The house, which used to hide its face behind a screen of mature pines and Monterey cypress (*Cupressus macrocarpa*), now looks out over a tangled mass of wind-felled trees. At the Conrah Hotel in Chancery it was the old beeches which took the full force of the storm. While many still remain, several great trees crashed on to the main road and driveway, their shallow roots lifting the soil around them. Evergreen trees such as a large holly and a Scots pine were also uprooted. The damage to the under-planting of rhododendrons and azaleas will take time to repair after the great beech boles are cut up and carted away.

On the younger University campus at Aberystwyth the mixed plantings of pine species performed well in their designated function as shelter belts on the windy hill. Most tossed and flexed in the wind, losing only small lengths of branches from their boughs. However, some individuals snapped or tore from the ground, and University gardeners report fifty-seven trees lost to the wind, chiefly pines and a few evergreen oaks burdened with the extra wind resistance of their winter leaves.

Older pines, often bordering roads or paths, suffered more severely, wrenched apart at twenty feet or more above ground, where the trunk bifurcates to support the crown. Scots pine (*Pinus sylvestris)* and the tall black pine (*Pinus nigra),* as on Plas Crug Avenue, seem particularly prone to this sort of damage. Others, such as the more globular-shaped specimen tree of the cluster pine (*Pinus pinaster)* in Llangorwen churchyard, simply rolled over, its shallow roots unable to sustain the buffeting on the dense foliage above.

Such losses to the landscape badly need to be replaced. Scots pines used to act as ancient way markers on the roads of rural Cardiganshire, while that cluster pine has been a landmark in scores of wedding photographs. It is important to adopt at least a hundred-year vision when planting a tree.

1990

Sculptural foliage in the spring garden

While it is traditional to greet snowdrops and daffodils as the symbols of spring, even greater admiration is due to the sculptural herbaceous plants which have cheered us through the winter and are now opening their intricately ornamental flower heads.

Two plant families are foremost in my esteem at this time of year, the hellebores and the euphorbias, herbaceous plants whose winter foliage is green and frost-resistant; rimed in hoar frost or topped with snow, they contribute form and elegance at a time when all else in the border is dried and dead.

Flowering now is the Lenten rose, *Helleborus orientalis*, far more beautiful and less plastic in appearance than the well-known Christmas rose, *Helleborus niger*.

The Lenten rose comes from Greece, and passes the winter as a clump of glossy green leaves. Towards January, as these age and blacken at the margins, they can be cut away, soon to be replaced by a neat clump of flower heads some twelve inches tall, each branching to bear three or four nodding buds resting, like a winter aconite, upon a collar of a five-pointed young leaf. The first flowers are open now, deeply bowl-shaped in greenish cream mottled at the petal bases with liverish red and focused on a huge boss of stamens shaped like little paddles. Other cultivars have wine-red flowers or an intermediate dusty pink.

Helleborus argutifolius also warmed the winter with its leathery, spiny-margined three-lobed leaves and is now decked with contrasting buds of pale yellow-green. *Helleborus foetidus,* meanwhile, a native plant of Britain and Europe, is in full bloom, the narrow eight-fingered dark green foliage topped by a shower of new growth. The winter-grown flower head, in pale, pale green, rears twelve inches above the foliage, a shower of up to fifty nodding, five-petalled bells, each touched at the rim with a hint of red. 'Foetidus' seems a slanderous name for this plant. While not deeply fragrant, the worst it can offer, even as a cut flower, is the slightly acrid scent of broad beans, not a remotely rotting smell.

The euphorbias are in the main still gathering themselves up to flower. *Euphorbia myrsinites* looks especially well in rockeries or pots, where the trailing stems reach out, densely clothed in dull, milky-green leaves. The terminal shoots each hold a nest of rusty-red eggs composed of tightly closed bracts which, had the weather been milder, would already have developed to an acid yellow.

Bigger species are *Euphorbia robbiae,* a rampant, robust shrubby plant which makes immaculate mounded clumps of dark laurel-green even in a poor shady border, and *Euphorbia characias wulfenii*, a native of the western Mediterranean which grows to four feet in a rich border. Both now bear their future flower heads, nodding over like umbrella handles on the top of each leafy stem.

However, the winter accolade must surely be awarded to the slender biennial *Euphorbia lathyris* or caper spurge, whose single tall erect stems bear rows of narrow green leaves arranged geometrically to point outwards like the four points of the compass. Each leaf midrib is a contrasting white. When the flowers appear in July they are scarcely worthy of remark, but only by awaiting the explosive distribution of the seeds in autumn can this elegant alleged mole-repellent be perpetuated around the garden.

1992

Camellias

Camellias are appearing in the garden shops now, usually bearing exquisite large red, pink or white flowers among their glossy dark green leaves. In time they should grow to become large shrubs or small trees. But why, I wonder, does one so seldom see a camellia blooming as beautifully in a suburban garden? I went along to visit Colin Morgan's spectacular shrub garden near Aberystwyth to find out.

The first requirement of a camellia is a rich, acid soil. Soil pH should be no problem to any of us here, but organic rich soil is another matter. Leaf mulch in copious quantities is the answer. Colin Morgan's camellias have a deep mulch of deciduous tree leaves heaped around their bases, providing ample forage for the many blackbirds tirelessly leaf-turning in search of food. He keeps this mulch regularly replenished to a depth of several inches from a giant heap kindly supplied in autumn by the council roadsweepers.

Secondly, camellias must not dry out. Although they will not tolerate a waterlogged soil, they may need watering during a dry summer unless planted in a reliably moist situation.

Thirdly, shade is vital. One of the best situations is to grow your camellia on a north wall (provided it is also sheltered from wind) or else in shaded and sheltered woodland. The flowers are sensitive to frost—and this fact might lead you to plant your lovely, new, green-house reared camellia in a warm and sunny spot. Not wise: it is the early sun striking the frosted petals which produces a rapid and damaging thaw and dead or discoloured blooms. Nestling in the lee of a north wall or in deep woodland shade, the air temperature will rise slowly from freezing as the day progresses, and the frozen buds and blooms will gently thaw with a minimum of damage. One shrub gardener, Sybil Emberton, in her book *A Year in the Shrub Garden* writes of setting the alarm clock for dawn on frosty mornings in order to dash out with the watering can to thaw with cold water the frosted buds before the sun can reach them! Evening wraps of net curtain or Rokolene may also do the trick, but these are the activities of the real enthusiasts. For the camellia which must take care of itself, the choice of setting is all important.

Many of the ornamental camellias are varieties of *Camellia japonica*, whose principal drawback is that dead flower heads are retained on the bush. Others are hybrids involving *Camellia japonica* and *Camellia reticulata* or *Camellia saluensis*. The hybrid *Camellia x williamsii* varieties have the advantage that they drop ageing blooms as more appear. Colin, who sells his excess plants through David Frost's stall in Aberystwyth Market Hall, showed me the exquisite pink-flowered hybrid 'Donation' and the delicate apple-blossom-pink 'J. C. Williams'. He has fine specimen plants of *Camellia japonica* 'Adolphe Audusson', which has brilliant red flowers reminiscent of the tropical hibiscus, and of *Camellia japonica* 'Magnoliaeflora', which is notable as much for its beautiful glossy green foliage and luxuriant growth form as for its white but weather-sensitive flowers.

So is a camellia suitable for you? Perhaps the real question is are you suitable for a camellia? Unless you can offer an appropriate situation and tender loving care and mulch in the coming years, you might really be happier relaxing with a soothing infusion of *Camellia sinensis*, otherwise known as a cup of tea!

1989

Rubbing salt in the wound

Anyone who watched the sea on January 5 this year will long remember the crashing waves and the plumes of spray floating away inland like smoke from a fire.

On the Aberystwyth promenade the waves broke with such force against the sea wall in front of Alexandra Hall that huge bomb-bursts of white water completely obscured the building, spreading out into separate trails of water each returning comet-like to earth.

From the crown of each explosion a white mist of spray drifted over the rooftops, evaporating into invisibility as it went. Little wonder that gardeners detected salt damage to plants and shrubs as far as twelve miles inland, and everyone looked indistinctly out through salt-rimed window panes.

Privet and euonymus scorch and blacken on their windward sides but will recover their appearance with the new growth of spring. Leyland cypresses also suffer salt damage and may make a less complete recovery. It is noticeable that the tall specimens in the University's Botany Garden on Penglais Hill have chronically distorted and browned tops now that their height extends above the sheltering lee of the hill and catches the blast of airborne salt.

Most deciduous trees may be expected to be unaffected, the salt washed away by rain before the sensitive buds began to burst, but there is both a salt and winter-chill set-back to Aberystwyth bedding schemes. John Shipman, Ceredigion DC Horticultural and Landscape Officer, reports salt-scorched leaves on the pansies and polyanthus, and even some deaths among the wallflowers in the Castle Grounds.

Where the spring bulb displays on the promenade are concerned, only time will show how well they withstood their January sousing. Last winter's storms came three weeks later, washing out many of the seafront daffodils, and destroying the fleshy stems of all those exposed to the salt-laden blast. At the time of this year's dousing the bulbs were still establishing their roots but not yet reaching to the light. John Shipman remains cautiously optimistic: in other seasons the winter bulbs have had a similar dousing with gravel and sea water, yet all has been well for St David's Day. The wrecked daffodil displays of 1990 were the first such disaster in thirteen years.

As the Siberian cold settles upon us, salt from another source threatens some trees and flowers. Although a cheap and efficient way to clear icy roads, the salt run-off can poison roadside trees and be sprayed by vehicle wheels into adjoining gardens.

In Belgium, salt damage to trees is taken so seriously that road gritting is now done purely with sand and gravel.

There are other less damaging chemicals. Calcium magnesium acetate is kinder to plants but can cause skin and bronchial problems in people. Urea is already used on parts of the M6 motorway, but decomposes malodorously to ammonia. Both chemicals are more expensive: twice the bulk is needed for road treatment, at twenty times the price of salt. Where grit can be a sufficient solution, it seems by far the least troublesome option.

1991

Designs on our wallets

Garden design, we are told by BBC2's recent six-part series on the subject, is at a crossroads. New vistas and innovations beckon; greater changes are in the offing than anything since Capability Brown.

It is a crossroads, however, at which I am tempted to turn back. Out, in this brave future, goes time as the gardener's chief ally, and in with a vengeance comes money, thousands and thousands of pounds of it. I do not recollect seeing one of these fashionable designers planting a sapling with a view to its eventual appearance as a spreading tree.

The new slogan of describing the garden as 'the outdoor room' is designed to soften us up to the idea of buying plants and 'hard landscaping' as we might buy carpets and the three-piece suite. All is installed by professionals in a matter of weeks, and we simply mosey down to the garden centre to pick out a few co-ordinating terracotta pots, and perhaps a sculpture or two to emphasise our social position.

Doubtless we shall also be encouraged to tire of our 1990s gardens within the decade, and again to employ a fleet of professionals to rip it up and start again. In any case, by that time many of the handsome and expensive pot-grown shrubs with which the instant garden was furnished will have grown to a mature size and need to be destroyed. As several designers remarked, plants are the backdrop; we do not organise the garden around its plants, but vice versa.

Humour—usually that of the designer—is deemed another essential feature of contemporary design, and here again I sense a commercial motive. Visual jokes in a public or demonstration garden are all very well; an endless stream of humanity shuffles through the Exhibition Gardens at Chelsea, and the joke is a huge success. Moreover, in less than a week it is demolished.

However, I can think of few jokes unlikely to stale on daily acquaintance. Indeed, to live looking out, year after year, on the same pastiche is more likely to promote the sort of humour of which the proprietor is the butt. Is this perhaps the idea? Just as ripping out and redesigning fitted kitchens was the great folly of the last decade, fuelled by rapid change in fashionable knobs, hobs and worktops, so we are now being lured, chequebook in hand, into the garden.

Gardening presently holds a high position in the rank of British recreations and, like that other top hobby, fishing, it is an inexpensive and stress-reducing activity. Traditional gardening is all about patience, and the satisfaction derived from nurturing plants, coaxing them along from small beginnings (often gifts from friends or neighbours), and knowing the biography of the individual plants in the garden. It offers the satisfaction which comes from a small act of creation.

The new gardener on his architect-designed patio is more likely to be fiddling with his laser-lights control panel, or flicking through his monthly plant maintenance handbook: 'Plants B12, C17, C37—trim in July'. If the gardening urge is strong he will set off to the garden centre to buy yet more accessories or pots.

Probably the last thing he might do is dig or weed, for his tiny £10,000 garden will be two-thirds interesting paving tastefully margined in easy-care ground-covering perennials and shrubs forbidding to any kind of interference. Still, it gives him all the more time to work up his stress levels in the pursuit of yet more wealth with which to purchase up-to-date garden technology and style.

1991

march

Perfection in yellow, green and blue

Each year I am delighted anew by the natural harmony of the early spring flowers. There is no jarring note; all the principal elements of the spring garden are shades of yellow, clean new green, or the smallest touches of brilliant blue. Daffodils, where they avoided the damaging salt spray of recent storms, are looking beautiful. I love best those closest relations of the wild Lent lily in which the golden trumpet is enhanced by the translucency of the pale yellow wings of the flower.

Hugging the ground on banks and in woodland gardens are drifts of wild primroses, their clear pale yellow blooms shining out even in the dusk or by moonlight while neighbouring polyanthus merge in low light into obscurity. Looming above them are the handsome greenish-yellow trusses of *Helleborus argutifolius* and the early green flowers of *Euphorbia rigida*. Further harmonies in green are provided by the trailing grey-blue foliage and yellow bracts of *Euphorbia myrsinites* and the striking greenish-white buds adorning the bay, *Laurus nobilis*.

Piquant contrasts of sharp blue are provided by the elegant little grape hyacinths pushing up through mats of mossy saxifrage, and the blooms of lungwort, *Pulmonaria saccharata,* which first open pink and then mature to a clear forget-me-not blue.

Softer shades of blue are contributed by the wide open blooms of periwinkle, *Vinca major*, and the smokier blue of rosemary, which has been flowering tirelessly since December. In deeper shade, forget-me-not blue appears again in a haze of tiny white-eyed flowers borne on *Brunnera macrophylla*. At this time of year the leaves are small and light green; in summer the plant takes on a very different appearance with huge heart-shaped dark green leaves providing a lush undergrowth and weed-excluding ground cover.

Among the yellow company of spring there is another enormously appealing member, that little wildflower the lesser celandine, *Ranunculus ficaria*, whose petals open at every hint of sunshine to expose an extraordinary reflective brilliance. I love this little flower, but introduce it to your garden with caution for it is extremely difficult to control. In flower beds it will readily spread to form an impenetrable mat and is very difficult to weed. One's only chance is to set about the poor plant in early spring while it is bearing its lovely blooms. At this time it holds together fairly well and can be weeded out with a bit of care.

Later in the season any attempt to displace a lesser celandine will leave countless small swollen tubers, each about the size of a grain of wheat, each destined to grow next year to a new plant. It is through this method of spread that celandines positively welcome disturbed ground and spring up with great enthusiasm the following year. There are cultivars of *Ranunculus ficaria*. The variety 'Flore-pleno' has double flowers and is said to be non-invasive and clump-forming. However, feeling that the single flower can scarcely be improved upon, I have not tried it myself.

1990

Tree planting—whips or stakes?

It is a paradox not apparent to many amateur gardeners that the simple route to a healthy and substantial tree is not necessarily to buy the largest container-grown sapling to be found. Instead it may be better to plant small, insignificant 'whips', young spindly trees up to two feet in height, and allow a little longer for them to grow. Small trees, once their roots are well established, grow at a prodigious rate, whereas larger ones may be severely set back by their move.

Pot-grown trees readily become root-bound, their roots trained around and around within the confines of the pot and reluctant to reach rapidly out into the surrounding soil. Vibration from the wind in the branches further discourages invasive new roots by joggling the pot-shaped lump of peat in its hole and breaking new rootlets trying to cross the boundary.

The attractive branches, when fully leafed, may demand more moisture than the compact root system can collect, and without careful watering, the first season can convert the shapely and expensive tree into a cripple, with lopsided die-back forever spoiling its symmetry.

Rich feeding with soil improved with compost, manure and peat, careful staking and attentive watering are the skills which prevent these horrors, and are the essential after-care for the instant garden. Our finest native trees, however, spring from very different origins and the less demanding techniques for planting small bare-rooted trees have a place in our gardens.

Planting of bare-rooted trees should be completed between November and April, when the buds are dormant and root activity can precede the demands of leaf growth. A wide range of native and ornamental species are obtainable from mail-order tree nurseries at a fraction of the pot-grown prices. They will arrive in bundles, polythene-wrapped, and if the weather is too inclement for planting, they should be unwrapped and heeled in as a bundle at an angle of 45° until the opportunity for planting arises.

Now as the soil warms is an excellent time to slot in a few trees either in the garden or on any spare scrap of land. Cut out a square of turf one and a half spade widths wide and dig out the soil to a spit's depth. Remove the bare-rooted whip from its bundle, dip the roots in a bucket of water, and position it vertically in the hole. Crumble in the soil about the roots. Then divide the turf square in two with the spade and stamp them back—upside down to kill the grass—in the hole. By this simple method a small copse is rapidly planted, and can be thinned in subsequent years to make room for the nicest trees.

Where staking is deemed necessary (and in the case of pot grown trees and larger saplings in windswept situations it will be), recent research has rejected the long-accepted use of a tall stake attached at three points on its length to the sapling tree. Flexing in the wind is now known to be necessary to young trees' healthy development, creating a strong and tapering trunk well anchored in the ground. Wind is damaging when the plant rocks enough to strain on its roots, but too-carefully staked trees may later snap in the wind.

Tree specialists now believe that the purpose of protecting the establishing roots is better served by a short stake not more than one third of the height of the tree, and belted to it near the top. Even this should not remain for more than eighteen months while the young tree finds its feet.

1991

Taking giant steps up the mountain

The outlook from the Corris Craft Centre Cafe, one of those strange beehives of glass adjoining the long straight road out of Corris, is dominated by forbiddingly steep mountains. The old slate town of Corris nestles almost invisible in the valley, and beyond it the mountain rises at an achingly consistent steepness, a patchwork of bracken, heather and open scree.

The observant tourist may notice an area of woodland clothing the lower slopes and remark upon its mixture of deciduous and evergreen trees, in contrast to the uniform forestry plantations nearby. It is unlikely though, that he will realise he is looking at a remarkable garden, star of *Gardener's World* in 1985 both for plantsmanship and for one man's landscaping skills.

Mrs Dorothy Paish still lives at Brynhyfryd and tends the garden which she and her husband began to create in 1961. Except for a Douglas fir and three graceful mature beeches by the house, it then lacked distinction as a garden, while behind the house the boulder-strewn mountain reared at an uncompromising angle.

Not satisfied with terracing and planting the lower levels around the house, David Paish was lured ever farther up the mountain, reclaiming the land from its poisonous bracken, planting exotic rhododendrons, conifers and banks of heather. He landscaped the hillside with zigzag trails, on which one walks single file, and with an infinite number of steps robustly built of the copious slabs of native stone which lie all around. There is not a trace of cement, not a chisel mark, timber riser or handrail.

This landscaping has a timeless quality born of the simple technology which created it—a crowbar, a shovel and a good eye for a slab! Nine years of path-building is represented here, giving gentle access to four acres of preciptous hillside, now richly grown with acid-loving shrubs and trees. It is a retirement garden to strike awe into the young: its architect commenced the task at the age of fify-nine.

When I visited the garden in early March, there were already rhododendrons in bloom, the frilly white flowers of *Rhododendron moupinense* speckled pink on the topmost petal, and another handsome bush *Rhododendron* 'Nobleanum Venustum' decked in a stronger pink.

Cutting and pruning

The recent fine weekend took me out into the garden reviewing the greening skeletons of the winter garden. Many of these skeletons required a severe pruning, and with the detachment that the winter's musing allows, I have steeled myself for the total destruction of two trees, a dangerously leaning apple tree, dislodged in a previous winter storm, and a sadly lopsided aspen.

This is certainly the time to implement such drastic changes, before the buds have broken and the trees look heart-breakingly pretty in fresh pink apple blossom and delicately crimped, wobbling, copper-tinted aspen leaves. There is space, too, for a bonfire now where soon young vegetables will be occupying the plot.

My first attack was on the butterfly bush, *Buddleia davidii*, whose spindly last year's canes were already sprouting silvery green stars of new leaves. Ruthlessly I cut it back to within three feet of the ground, knowing stronger new growth will soon spring out from below the cuts. Feeling even more remorseless, I moved on to the late-flowering *Clematis tangutica* and cut away, with shears and secateurs, the whole overhanging tangled head which overflows from the top of the trellis. All winter it has charmed the eye with old-man's-beard clocks of seeds, shining silvery in the weak sunlight. Soon it was bowling round the garden in the gusty dry wind.

Pausing briefly to behead the hydrangeas, I moved my savage clippers on to the wisteria, and here I am locked in a struggle with this maddening plant. I bought, nine years ago, a grafted *Wisteria sinensis*, which, if the experts are to be believed, should have soon flowered, the grafted material having, as it were, a built-in maturity predisposing flowering. In the icy January of 1984 it died, and throughout that summer the stump stood dead and discouraging. When, in the summer of 1985, new wisteria tendrils emerged from the rootstock below ground, I was so delighted I allowed it to ramp quite uncontrolled up the wall. So, I imagined, it would rapidly regain strength. I got what I deserved for this lack of early discipline, a tangle of jungly stems, a rich crown of feathery dark green summer foliage and never, as yet, a flower. Twice-yearly pruning is said to concentrate the shoots to form flower buds, and this involves further shortening every stem pruned last summer. This weekend it received a truly avenging 'short back and sides'. If this, too, fails, I shall next year cut away most of the vertical stems and start again in trying to produce a disciplined creeper.

Innovation as well as destruction is easier at this time of year, and I am planning some terraces and a path to add character to a piece of sloping, lightly shaded, back garden. Other beds and borders could be improved by greater width and more interesting shape. Next tool in my armoury is the spray bottle of Roundup or Tumbleweed. I first model the new border outline with a stretch of garden hose until I have defined the shape. An application of Roundup to the grass within the future border will have it dead and ready for digging in two to three weeks' time.

1993

The rare Derwydd daffodil

What makes a beautiful daffodil? For long I have held a particular fondness for the wild daffodil, *Narcissus pseudonarcissus*, in which the golden trumpet or corolla tube is surrounded by five pale yellow radiating petals. It is blooming now, as a wildflower in the woods around Llanerchaeron, often stunted to a modest six inches in height. It grows, too, in my garden, as naturalised clumps probably dating from the early years of the house's hundred-year history. This species of daffodil constituted the host of dancing daffodils espied by William Wordsworth during his cloud-like wanderings.

Double daffodils have enjoyed a more varied press. Steven Anderton writing recently in *The Times* described them as having all the charm of a sucked orange. However, an old-fashioned bright yellow double is widespread locally in cottage gardens and churchyards dating from Victorian or much earlier times. It is usually identified as 'Van Sion' or 'Telemonius Plenus'. The corolla is split almost to its base and encircles a dense arrangement of strongly yellow petaloids. The look of the wild ancestor is retained in the several whorls of five paler, pointed petals which contribute to the paper-windmill appearance of the flower. It was obviously widely planted in the past and for some people today this is still the traditional Welsh garden daffodil. Sometimes the flower has a somewhat greenish hue and this has led to debate among botanists as to whether it is in fact the ancient Welsh rarity, the Derwydd daffodil.

Derwydd daffodils sound nothing to brag about. Alan Stepney Gulstan Esq., of Derwydd, writing in the *Transactions of the Carmarthenshire Antiquarian Society and Field Club* of 1907 describes the 'Virescent dwarf double daffodil of Derwydd' as having grown in profusion in the area for more than two hundred years. Other authors use the term 'degenerate'. So last week in wind and rain an expedition was mounted to scour the meadows in the vicinity of Llandeilo to meet the virescent dwarf on its home ground.

We found it locally in several places, growing in sheep-grazed pasture, on sharply draining slopes on the wet red soil of the Old Red Sandstone. It was gratifyingly different from the familiar old double daff of our area. The buds, while still sheathed, point upwards and are as fat and globular as an allium bud. The spathe unfurls to reveal a thoroughly green many-segmented bud. The flower when it opens is dishevelled in the extreme, many of the longer petaloids distorted and ribbon-shaped, the centre a twisted mass of distinctly green petaloids, often arranged lopsidedly around several centres. Slugs seem to have an unusual fondness for the blooms, which are often damaged in bud, further contributing to the irregularity of the greenish-yellow flower.

While never likely to win any medals at a flower show, this degenerate little daffodil has a certain charm, robustly withstanding the ravages of wind and sheep in the open meadows where it has grown for at least 300 years. Modern scientists suggest it may be a mutant form of the Tenby daffodil, *Narcissus pseudonarcissus obvallaris*. However, Stepney Gulstan recorded, in 1907, that once collected and 'cultivated in the same soil for a few years, Derwydd daffodils rapidly assimilate a like appearance, and from flowers virescent and ragged, more nearly approach the beauty of Telemonius Plenus.' Perhaps the hardship of the Welsh hills is the sole cause of its unique appearance.

The National Trust garden at Llanerchaeron, is establishing a reference collection of daffodil varieties. A specimen of the Derwydd daffodil will be on display.

1995

april

Magical properties of manure

If there is a truly timeless preoccupation of gardeners, it is on the subject of composts and manures. As a rejuvenator of soils and promoter of fruitfulness their properties sometimes appear little short of miraculous. Christian gardeners may take their instruction from an apposite little parable, Luke 13: 6-9, in which the vineyard owner expresses his disgruntlement with a fig tree: 'Behold these three years I come seeking fruit on this fig tree and find none:—cut it down! Why doth it cumber the ground?'

The gardener replies, 'Lord let it alone this year also, till I shall dig around it and dung it. If it bear fruit thenceforth, *well*, but if not thou shalt cut it down.'

St Luke does not record whether the fig tree in question responded to this treatment with a bountiful crop of fruit, but the odds are good that it did. Two of the gardener's most time-honoured aids, patience and manure, were wisely employed to give the young fig the maturity and nutrients for fruiting.

The quality of patience has changed little over two millennia except to become in shorter supply. Increasingly gardeners want rapid results, we buy plants rather than seeds, fruit trees already on the point of fruiting, huge ornamental shrubs adorned with flowers, gadgets and products to speed and facilitate every task.

The subject of dung, meanwhile, has become both complex and sanitized. This gardening basic now comes in a mystifying range of guises, pre-bagged at the garden centre. Cow dung is processed to produce a crumbly sterilized, deodorized and concentrated medium such as '6X' or 'Cowpact'; chicken droppings appear as all-purpose organic fertilizer in neat brown cylindrical extruded pellets. Human excrement, too, finds its way into composts, a by-product of advanced sewage treatment but seldom explicitly named as an ingredient. Every product seems to work out as costing in the region of 5p per square yard at manufacturers' recommendations; what varies is the ratio of bulk to nutrients.

Gardeners satisfied with their soil structure need look no further than a tonic application of Growmore granules, which deliver equal proportions of nitrogen, phosphorus and potassium, 7 per cent of each in an inert medium. While sometimes decried as not organic, I find this distinction odd when the mineral deposits are themselves often of animal origin. However, infected by Geoff Hamilton's organic enthusiasm, I recently used pelleted chicken manure as a top dressing and discovered an unadvertised drawback. Moistened by a light sprinkling of rain, these inoffensive pellets emitted a sudden and powerful bouquet of chicken-farm.

The bulky manures and composts offer greater soil conditioning and less nutrients, usually around 1 per cent, of N, P and K by weight. The plant fibre improves the soil texture and its ability to retain water and dissolved nutrients. The goodness of Growmore quickly washes out of organic-poor soils. All these processed products are cleaner and more pleasant to handle than farmyard manure.

However, the old-fashioned product remains an economical option, especially in country areas: a trailer load can often be obtained for little more than the price of a bag or two of 6X. For larger gardens, it still makes good sense, especially if stored in a heap for a further year before use to ensure that it is thoroughly decayed. This precaution avoids the risk of nitrogen depletion when insufficiently rotted manure deprives the plants of nitrogen as a consequence of bacterial action in the manure. It also diminishes the macabre impact of organic bonuses like the dead sheep which arrived in our recent load of dung!

1993

A botanist's seaside garden

Gardening in the teeth of salt-laden winds is a challenge many gardeners feel they can do without, and they choose their home locations accordingly. Others, on finding themselves perched on windswept cliffs with a magnificent view, give in too easily, as the unrelieved grass around their properties will testify. Perhaps the rapid death of a few unwise purchases has convinced them of the futility of all attempts at creating a garden.

Seaside gardeners do have to limit themselves to plants capable of withstanding these conditions and their first priority must be creating shelter, for having done so a surprising number of plants will thrive in its lee. Secondly they must be patient, for growth rates may be vastly slowed. I have been admiring the wind-pruned beech hedge which sweeps theatrically up and inward at the front margin of Arthur Chater's Aberystwyth garden. It is about six feet tall and composed of a closely planted row of trees whose trunks range from six to twelve inches in girth. This hedge was planted sixty years ago by Arthur's father. In more favourable inland locations a specimen sixty-year-old beech tree would be expected to be some five feet in circumference!

The garden surrounding 'Windover' faces the harbour at just the point at which the picket fence gate frames the breaking waves as they roll lazily into the harbour mouth. The wind howls in off the sea, over the sloping crown of beeches, up the concrete drive and past the ivy-clad bungalow to the bare slopes of Pendinas. Some shrubs, such as box and daisy bush, *Olearia,* indicate their stress by their inelegant leaflessness on the windward side, but for the most part, as one would expect of a botanist who has many things to do other than cosset his garden, Arthur Chater's plants are fully resistant in their location.

A dominant feature of the garden is the several mature bushes of *Skimmia japonica.* This shrub invariably looks unbelievably neat and spruce, with its dense habit, leathery green leaves, waxy white buds and long-lasting holly-red berries. Birds do eat them, but without undue enthusiasm, so at this time of year skimmias look their best, with dense panicles of white flowers just opening and red berries still gleaming among the leaves. This shrub comes in two sexes, so it is important to have both male and female individuals. Blazing in the small lawn, the sunburst twigs of a severely pollarded willow, *Salix alba* 'Britzensis', form a halo of rich orange red. As the leaves come out, Arthur will cut the stems back to the gnarled goblet-shaped trunk to promote a new crown of young twigs for next year.

Another well-tried seaside shrub is *Euonymus japonicus.* It is perhaps the front hedge tree of Victorian seaside guest houses, but no longer so fashionable in the fickle market of the garden centre. At Windover, a hedge of it encloses a small 'private garden' to one side, and grows luxuriantly thick and tall to enclose a garden room roofed by the boughs of a white poplar. Up through the dark green evergreen leaves scramble several choice clematis, and a rambler rose. The room within is too shady for grass, and is floored with bluebells, crocus and celandine. Most delightful of all, there are, in this dense unmanaged shade, plants of an unusual wildflower, spurge laurel, *Daphne laureola*. As its name implies, it looks like a leggy spurge, but bears inconspicuous clusters of scented yellow-green four-lobed tubular flowers. Enclosed in this private garden one feels entirely remote from the sea, the house and indeed the world.

1995

Gwyn grows prize vegetables

Over the years, Gwyn Royle has built himself a reputation as one of the grand old men of competitive vegetable gardening, a reputation which now extends far beyond Talybont and his retirement village of the last seven years, Penrhyncoch. The corner cupboard is packed to capacity with cups and trophies from the show benches, and like an elder statesman of his hobby he now judges as frequently as he competes, at shows throughout the county. Since the beginning of the year he has attracted a growing following of listeners through his appearance as a regular guest of Selwyn Jones on Radio Ceredigion's *Am Ddeg*, Tuesdays at 10 am.

Although registered disabled, Gwyn at 65 still maintains a highly productive and perfectly tended plot behind the modern bungalow he shares with his wife Mai, a former secretary of the Talybont Show. Rising in the morning, it is his enduring pleasure to look out of the bedroom window on faultless rows of onions, potatoes, carrots, parsnips and shallots, and the brook burbling by at the garden's end. The previous owner had laid her garden to shrubs, grass and an ornamental pond. Gwyn soon cleared it back to provide the raw material of his skill, a neat stone-free weedless rectangle of soil.

That soil spent the winter under black polythene, protected from excessive leaching of the nutrients by winter rain, and from the waterlogging so prevalent this spring. Only on 19 March did he draw back the wraps and commence planting. When I visited before Easter, the onions and shallots were already in the ground, the bottle-necked shallots actually crowned with eager tufts of green leaves, for these had been brought on in the conservatory before being planted out. The conservatory staging was fully occupied, tiny tomato plants emerging from the sieved compost, other seeds yet to germinate, and boxes of the serious competitor's potatoes, 'Kestral', 'Winston' and 'Nadine', sprouting darkly in the daylight.

What I came especially to see was the nurturing ground for those absurdly long, perfectly formed carrots and parsnips. Immediately below Gwyn's window is a row of big oil drums, bottomless now and filled with builders' sand. Within each he forces three holes some six inches in diameter by pressing down with an iron rod which lives in the garden shed for this purpose alone. Boring full five feet deep, into the soil beneath the drums, he then fills each hole, gently and carefully, with The Mixture, carefully firming it down. On my visit he had already planted the parsnips, a group of three seeds at the top of each column of growing medium, protected from the elements by a clear plastic collar cut from a soft drinks bottle, or a plastic pint from the beer tent. Two seedlings will be weeded out to allow one single plant to prosper in each column.

For the first time in print, Gwyn's family recipe (son Eric is also a champion vegetable grower) is offered to the public. The growing medium is composed of equal parts of soil, sand and peat. To each eight gallons of this is added 4 oz lime, 2 oz sulphate of potash, 4 oz superphosphate, sieved through a kitchen sieve, 4 oz calcified seaweed, 2 oz bonemeal, and 2 tablespoons Bromophos or Chlorophos to deter the carrot rootfly. The whole is mixed carefully like dry cement upon a board before it is poured into the holes.

Farmyard manure should never be used for root vegetables: the rich feeding is likely to encourage the root to divide in search of the nutrients instead of questing ever deeper underground. Only in midsummer, when the carrots have already reached their full length, does Gwyn introduce a foliar feed, home produced by steeping sheep's manure in an iron cauldron of water.

What induced Gwyn to reveal the secrets of his success? Perhaps partly his new role as gardening broadcaster, but more important, the hope that it may prompt new competitors to give this particular quest for excellence a try.

1994

Biological control of slugs

Was I alone in feeling slightly nauseous at the sight of sick slugs exploding on television, as was portrayed in one of last year's editions of *Gardeners World*? The product which brings about this vengeance upon the gardener's traditional enemy comes with fine and ecologically sound credentials; it is a form of biological control, specific to the slug, and thus allows us to avoid the organic gardener's bane, namely noxious chemicals about the garden.

Instead, we are to drench the soil with a suspension of six million parasitic nematode worms. These bore into the slugs and also infect them with a bacterium. The ensuing ravages of disease quenches the slug's appetite within a week and kills it in a fortnight. Looking closely, the gardener will detect the march of the disease in the form of hunchbacked slugs, their mantle bulbously swollen, pursuing their doomed progress around the garden.

The product is at present expensive and in short supply, so early ordering is recommended. Marketed as Nemaslug it can be obtained mail order from Defenders, PO Box 131, Ashford, Kent, TN25 5BR or from garden centres stocking the Zeneca's 'Nature's Friends' range of organic products. A pack of six million worms costs £13 and is sufficient to treat 20 square metres of ground. Provided the soil remains moist, it should remain infectious for six weeks. The worms are themselves living creatures and as such are vulnerable to damage. They remain in good condition in the packaging for just two to three days in a cool place or up to four weeks in the refrigerator. It is important to be at home when they are delivered and on good terms with the Post Office.

Limitations to the latest slug killer are that it is not found to be effective on snails, other than the generally inoffensive pond snail. As such it is not recommended for use near ponds. Also the parasitic worms rapidly die in too dry or in waterlogged soil, so perhaps a better application is in the vegetable garden rather than in the ornamental bog garden, home of slug-devastated *Ligularia*.

Death, even of slugs, is not pretty, and most of us would prefer not to notice it. Perhaps my feelings will change, but I can't help finding a slimy and sudden death beside the metaldehyde pellets less revolting than watching my garden slugs limping around for a fortnight in the likeness of the Hunchback of Nôtre Dame.

1994

Ambridge to Wil Akkermans, all in the Gardens Scheme

I have not myself acquired the habit of listening to 'The Archers', but am aware that for many of their vast audience they are as real as the next-door neighbours.

Reality and fantasy blur further with a wide variety of 'spin-off' events for Archers fans, 'Meet the Archers' holidays, and publicity events in which weddings and parties are acted out for the cameras. Although it remains a radio show, casting decisions are now made not merely upon voice quality but require that the voices are housed in plausible bodies for the characters they represent.

Plausible gardens are also called for in the year in which five Ambridge families join the National Gardens Scheme to open their gardens to the public. As is common in pretty English villages (and a few Welsh ones such as Kerry near Newtown and Talybont-on-Usk), the community charges a joint admission to the several separate and private gardens in one village.

At Ambridge, the Hall, Brookfield Farm, Grey Gables, The Lodge and Keepers' and Woodbine Cottages will be opening on Wednesday, 1

July. They have been recruited to the scheme by County Organizer, Mrs Phoebe Giddings-Wesley, of Lower Loxley in Borsetshire.

Publicity on 'The Archers' for real places and events is almost invariably welcome, though I do recollect indignation in Borth a few years ago when Tony Archer failed to enjoy his holiday there. In this case the Gardens Scheme organisers have certainly risen with delight to the opportunities, and have included the fictional Borsetshire in the 1992 edition of the 'Yellow Book'—properly entitled *Gardens of England and Wales*. The entry, which appears after Yorkshire in the England section, is preceded by an emphatic warning to overseas visitors that the gardens cannot be visited!

The Yellow Book is published annually and these days occupies a place in the top ten paperback best-sellers for about four months. Just to skim its pages brings out the latent sociologist in us all. How fascinating it would be to plan a tour encompassing the sixty-four Old Rectories, Old Parsonages and Old Vicarages opening to public view, or to visit Malvern Terrace, Barnsbury, London N1 where numbers 1, 2, 3, 4, 5, 6, 7, 8 and 10 will be simultaneously open to the public. What sort of people, one wonders, live at number 9?

Whether your sights are set on Sandringham, Sissinghurst or 33 Mundania Road, Peckham Rye, the Yellow Book provides concise descriptions and details of opening times, and an invaluable index by name of garden to help those whose grasp, like mine, of the counties is a little shaky.

The Yellow Book is an invaluable car companion. There is no backwater so remote that a reference to its pages may not turn up an exquisite cottage garden or a fine mansion worthy of a visit. Gardens which open by appointment are often very quiet and tranquil with hardly a visitor to be seen, while others, which offer limited opening days with teas and plant stalls, can be a major local event, drawing several hundred visitors.

In Ceredigion the extensively redesigned gardens at Llanllyr, and the wildlife garden at Winllan, both near Talsarn, have attracted large crowds on their official opening days. Equally popular with visitors is Carrog, Llanddeiniol, where veteran garden scheme members Mr and Mrs Geoffrey Williams will on 28 June receive a presentation of a trowel to mark their twenty-first year in the scheme.

A new entry this year is Wil Akkermans's garden at Cae Hir, Cribyn, near Lampeter, which will be open on two days in support of the scheme. I hear excellent reports of this garden which is designed upon a theme of three separate shrub gardens of red, yellow and blue created from rough grazing since 1985. The six-acre garden is a monument to the amount that can be achieved by one man with hand tools and a wheelbarrow. Mr Akkermans's garden is also open daily (except Mondays) throughout the summer.

1992

Mail-order purchasing or the CHS plant sale

Seduced by the colour photographs in a horticultural firm's spring catalogue, I sent off my £4.75 for three large-flowered poppies, *Papaver orientale* 'Mrs Perry', of an exquisite tissue-paper pink. 'Easy to grow', 'unfastidious as to soil'; my inner eye filled in three huge gaps in the mixed border. Full of similar optimism I added £4.95 for three young *Chrysanthemum pacificum*, a Japanese plant recently featured in the Royal Horticultural Society magazine *The Garden* for its silver-edged foliage, small tansy-like flowers, and extraordinary hardiness in the face of either frost or drought.

I was forced to reflect, on receiving my £10 worth of plants, that I would not so willingly have parted with money for them at a garden centre. The chrysanthemums seemed very small and puny, a single anaemic stem reaching towards the light. The poppies were simply three sprouting sections of root, each with a leaf base forming at one end. They will clearly need time and love before they fulfil their alleged promise. In time they probably will, but what I have bought is really just three small 2½-inch root cuttings from an established plant.

There are two conclusions to be drawn from this observation. One is that the high standard of presentation which we garden-centre shoppers have come to expect can be short-cut by mail-order companies provided that their plants do eventually grow. The other is that where the customer inspects before purchase, ugly-looking bits of plant do not command high prices.

This phenomenon can work in the purchaser's favour, and seldom better than at the Cardiganshire Horticultural Society's annual plant sale. This event, held in Llanfarian Village Hall, generally attracts a substantial press of shoppers waiting for the doors to open. As with a jumble sale, everyone streams inside in search of the bargains and trading is fast and furious. Within seconds the pot-grown azalea in flower or the primulas and pansies in bud will have been snapped up. But at this kind of jumble sale value is not necessarily correlated with visual impact. Fragments of root, tufts of foliage in re-used polythene bags retail not for pounds but for pence, but may hold enormous promise. These tufts and fragments have been carved off choice plants in local gardeners' gardens. They may look like nothing special but they are just as likely as (indeed more so than) my expensive 'Mrs Perry' to grow. Chunks of root may soon sprout a tree peony, odd corms a *Dierama pucherrima*, tufts of leafy rhizome an unusual iris.

Two years ago I came home with a tuft of narrow green strap-like leaves arranged in a fan, and the pencil label 'Libertia'. Now a handsome clump on the windy side of my garden, it produces, in early summer, small white flowers like three-pointed stars, tiered up long thin stems.

Another year, I remember the merchandise included a five-foot *Cornus mas* 'Variegata', a Rolls-Royce among garden shrubs, which had been evicted from a member's garden for failing, over several years, to flower as it should on bare winter twigs.

Less showy bargains abound. Useful garden ground coverers like dead-nettles, pulmonaria and the more ordinary euphorbias can be hard to find in garden centres, perhaps because they spread so well that a single purchase will supply a gardener for life. However, many a gardener is grateful to *Euphorbia robbiae* for bringing dark green weed-proof foliage and cheerful spring green flowers to that dark corner by the dustbins, or to the yellow archangel or the blue-starred greater periwinkle for smothering a difficult and shady bank. Every garden needs its unsung workhorses as well as its stars.

1991

Hawkstone—an eighteenth-century Disneyworld?

On a softly damp autumn day last year I visited Hawkstone Park near Hodnet in Shropshire in the company of a small group of Friends of Hafod. *Cognoscenti* of the eighteenth-century Picturesque movement in landscape design, they were better prepared than I for the day's excursion.

However, a quick perusal on the bus of Dr Samuel Johnson's diary entry of 1774 led me to expect to see 'the sublime, the dreadful and the vast', a landscape of 'terrific grandeur', 'the horrors of precipices, the awfulness of shades, inaccessible altitude and horrible profundity'. As we travelled by mini-bus across the flat, formless landscape north-east of Shrewsbury, it all seemed a bit unlikely and I wondered whether the famous diarist was prone to a spot of hyperbole. Certainly he was not above a spot of character assassination, describing Hawkstone House itself as 'magnificent compared with the rank of its owner'.

We did not visit the house, which is in separate ownership, but were met by Simon Walding, Landscape Architect, who had drawn up restoration plans for the landscape on behalf of Shropshire County Council and the Countryside Commission. As he conducted us around the area, he explained how the landscape now belonged with the Hawkstone Park Hotel and golf course, and had recently become the property of the immensely wealthy Barclay brothers, whose business interests include shipping and hotels in London and Monte Carlo. Eschewing grant aid, they had elected to finance the restoration themselves, and at a cost of some 2½ million pounds to open it to the public on completion. Listed as a Grade I landscape by English Heritage, Hawkstone Park is rated on a par with Blenheim in Oxfordshire.

We spent some four hours walking the sinuous footpaths through the wooded landscape, emerging to view outlooks, monuments, towers and follies. The key to Hawkstone's awesome profundity lies in the geology, a region of natural relief, where soft Permian sandstone rears above the regular patchwork of fields which stretch flatly away to the distant Welsh hills. The sandstone forms natural crags, some as much as 150 feet in height, and is moreover soft and easily carved. Mere scrabbling with the fingers will produce a trickle of sand. Eighteenth-century workmen readily embellished nature, carving rustic seats and shelters, tunnels through the rocky bluffs, an extensive grotto or artificial cave in the top of the scarp. As we toured the walks, stepping blindly into pitch-black tunnels, emerging at crags and follies, and ducking back into darkness, I felt increasingly like a field vole whose landscape is mapped by a network of tunnels broken by occasional dangerous excursions beneath the sky.

As the tour progressed one came to wonder whether great wealth does not perhaps produce excessive indulgence. Like an eighteenth-century Disneyworld, the Hawkstone attractions included a menagerie of animals, some living, others stuffed, picturesquely tended by 'Adam and Eve', and a visit to a cave manned by an automaton hermit. Other incongruous features included a Swiss Chalet, a Hawaiian Hut, a rustic alpine bridge. Perhaps most indulgent of all is Hawk Lake, designed by William Emes, a two-mile-long ribbon of water, held on the sloping landscape by a similarly lengthed embankment, entirely so that the Hills of Hawkstone could look out from their mansion upon the likeness of a river, and disport themselves in boats upon its surface.

1993

Fluctuating fashions in the tulip

It has long been fashionable to despise the municipal tulip, planted in regimented stands of a single colour, but I am delighted to see drab corners of Aberystwyth enlivened by beds of china-pink Lily-flowered tulips emerging from a froth of pale yellow wallflowers. This particularly lively colour combination is the epitome of spring cheerfulness, without the garishness which is possible with too much pillar-box red.

Tulips have been the subject of intensive selection and hybridization for nearly 400 years, and present a dazzling range of colour and form. It is possible to design a colour scheme and to flick through the shade-card range of the fourteen divisions of hybrid tulips till a perfect match can be found. Only a truly blue tulip has eluded the breeders; so-called blue tulips look thoroughly purple to me.

Seen in historical perspective, tulips—and indeed all plants—are splendidly cheap. In the mid-seventeenth century, as Dutch horticulturalists produced endless new hybrids from the Turkish and Caucasian species which had been shipped home to them, the tulip so caught the imagination of the wealthy that prices became extraordinarily inflated. Trading began in tulip futures, paper documents representing tulips yet to be propagated, and at the height of this speculation a single tulip could cost as much as a carriage and pair, or twelve acres of land. In modern terms, a tulip or a Porsche!

The trade, known in retrospect as 'tulipomania', reached ludicrous proportions with the wild bidding for a new red and white tulip called 'Semper Augustus' at a time when only two bulbs of the variety existed in Holland. There is a much repeated story, which certainly ought to be true, as to how one of these chanced to be purloined by a passing workman who, believing it to be an onion, consumed it with his fish supper and languished six months in gaol in consequence.

Ironically, these days the hybrid tulips raised in huge numbers by agribusinesses in East Anglia and the Netherlands are usually much cheaper than the species tulips which were among their ancestors.

Many of the wild tulips are endangered by changes in land use in their native terrain, and none should be collected from the wild without official permits. Specialist nurseries such as Broadleigh Gardens, Bishops Hull, Taunton, Somerset, will shortly be offering an extensive list of species and varieties among which the wild yellow *Tulipa batalinii* and the scarlet and black *Tulipa greigii* retail around £1 apiece, and the rare *Tulipa sprengeri* at £2.30. By seventeenth-century standards even these seem rather good value.

1990

Growing giant pumpkins

I was thumbing recently through the 1938 editions of *Country Life*, searching, as it happens, for the contemporary account of the forming of the terrace and paths at Trawsgoed mansion. What look like exceptionally large and thick paving slabs were in fact cast *in situ* out of concrete, false joints being created by the insertion of fillets of wood. This pioneering use of concrete, supervised by experts from The Cement and Concrete Association, was described in some detail in the commercial back pages of the magazine.

Drawn through the volume to browse, I was soon charmed to find a photograph of Mr H. Y. Nutt, of Radlett, posing proudly in plus fours beside a wheelbarrow containing his prizewinning 136 lb pumpkin. In his accompanying letter he waxed lyrical (if arithmetically inaccurate) as to the sums of money and poundage of pumpkin which might be generated if every one of its 334 seeds gave rise to a similar offspring!

It is often claimed that little changes in gardening, but Mr Nutt's pumpkin would look puny indeed beside the 500lb pumpkins routinely grown by Lincolnshire horticulturalist Bernard Lavery. His pumpkins need a fork-lift truck at least for their transportation, and he holds numerous records for largest vegetable in many categories.

Pumpkin strains have improved over the last fifty years, and the present world record of 891 lb is held by the elongate, orange-fleshed 'Atlantic Giant', which was developed in America. However a Rhydyfelin pumpkin enthusiast tells me he invariably gets his best results with 'Mammoth', a flatter golden globe whose symmetry is much prized at Hallowe'en.

It is now time to start pumpkin seeds in individual pots on the windowsill or in the greenhouse. Harden off outside as soon as the two oval cotyledon leaves are well developed. A larger indoor-grown plant may become soft and weak and whip around dangerously in high winds out in the vegetable patch. Pumpkins take up a lot of space, so only the two or three best seedlings are worth planting, each in soil on top of a trench filled with manure and straw. Another important rule is copious watering as the fruit enlarge. Not more than two should be allowed to develop on each plant.

Pumpkins for the local show bench do not win on size alone, but should be perfectly formed and symmetrical. The serious pumpkin grower regularly rotates the fruit upon its stem so that it will not be distorted by its own weight. He also makes an autumn visit to the osteopath—there is no ergonomically efficient way to lift a pumpkin!

1995

may

Brondanw, home of Clough Williams Ellis

Most people are familiar with the eccentric holiday village of Portmeirion, created since 1925 by Sir Clough Willliams Ellis, perhaps largely to entice his sophisticated London friends to undertake the arduous journey to the remote fastnesses of Wales. Here they were entertained in a luxurious hotel at the estuary shore, or lodged in the eclectic village in the gulley behind it. Modelled partly on the Italian fishing village of Portofino, it also incorporates a motley collection of classical replicas and other salvaged architectural oddments from around Britain. The concept is jokey, in a stage-set sort of way, with the campanile and pantheon packed improbably cheek by jowl. The vistas in the gardens may terminate in seats resembling a Punch and Judy stand, or an arbour composed of the sawn-off half of a clinker-built dinghy.

Visual jokes tend to pall if one sees them every day, and it makes a lot of sense to realize that the proud creator didn't actually live at Portmeirion, but in a seventeenth-century mansion, Plas Brondanw, tucked away in the hills behind Penrhyndeudraeth. Here he created, over his long life, a remarkable and very personal garden, more soothing to the spirit than his hectic village on the coast.

Arriving at Brondanw, one is immediately arrested by a single colour, a strong, aquamarine green, a shade most rare in plants. It appears on wrought iron gates, railings, garden furniture, and the distinctive little concave canopies of lead which deflect the rain above the doors of the various adjoining workers' cottages. Knobs, finials and the more intricate ironwork are further picked out in golden yellow. Set against the sober yew topiary, the hard furnishings of the garden, and they are numerous, stand out like children's toys scattered in an elegant drawing room.

The terraces below the house are divided into a number of garden rooms, bounded by beautifully trimmed yew or box, or a lattice of pleached limes. Each room contains a formal pond or sculpture, usually both. If the Italian cypress, *Cupressus sempervirens,* could be grown at Brondanw, I have no doubt Clough Williams Ellis would have grown them. Instead the many columnar elements evocative of Italian gardens are provided by fastigate yews wired into tight columns and trimmed to maintain a similar shape.

I particularly liked the circular garden beyond the house, from which one can, on a clear day, look up to the summit of Y Cnicht or out across a vista of rushy rough hill grass. Nestling within its sheltered perimeter are fine old Japanese azaleas as much as six feet tall, and, forming a grotto beneath the wall, a circular shaded pool which displays a single specimen marsh marigold, *Caltha palustris* 'Flore Pleno', gleaming theatrically against the darkness of its backdrop.

The house is closed up, but the gardens are carefully maintained and open daily for a modest fee. A visit would not be complete without an envigorating stroll up the hillside to The Tower, a folly subscribed for by Clough's brother officers in the Welsh Guards to mark his marriage in 1913 to Amabel Strachey. I suppose these days follies are subject to planning permission. Notwithstanding, perhaps the practice should be revived.

1994

The shady rockeries of Newby Hall

For most householders these days, a rockery is a small-scale structure, carefully constructed to mimic the sharp drainage and thin soil of an alpine scree slope, ornamented with random stones (very expensive these, if you buy them from a garden centre) and mulched, between the plants, with a layer of fine gravel. 'Alpines' represent a very substantial part of the plant trade, and a modern rockery has an entrancing range of plants, many of them low-growing and rosette- or mat-forming, derived not only from the Alps but from mountains farther afield such as in the Himalayas and South Africa.

The rockeries of the nineteenth century were very different in both scale and character. In the gardens of great houses they consisted of huge blocks of tumbled stone arranged in a landscape criss-crossed by rustic paths and perhaps leading to a focal point such as a statue, pool or grotto. Size of stones represented both opportunity and ostentation. At Chatsworth, Joseph Paxton (later to design the Crystal Palace) worked with blocks weighing as much as fifty tons, while at Pencarrow House in Cornwall massive weathered granite boulders were dragged, mainly downhill, from the neighbouring Bodmin Moor. In rockeries such as these you are unlikely to find a sempervivum or a raoulia—or, indeed, to notice one were it there. Trees, shrubs, ferns and other large foliage plants determine the character, often moist and bosky, of such rockeries. At Pencarrow House, little of the original exotic plantings remain except for one very old gnarled Japanese maple, *Acer palmatum dissectum*, now some eight feet tall and with a fine head of delicately cut green leaves.

Newby Hall, near Ripon, Yorkshire, has a well maintained extensive rockery of local sandstone, which descends to a boulder-strewn pool with balanced stone bridges. When summer borders are bright with colour all in the rockery is green and leafy: Solomon's seal, *peltiphyllums* bergenia, hart's tongue and buckler ferns give contrasting form and texture in the shade of mature trees.

On a recent spring visit I found the rockery much more colourful and the tree canopy still barely in leaf. The heavily scented brilliant yellow *Mahonia aquifolium* and orange-flowered *Berberis darwinii* grew luxuriantly among the rocks, and here and there were large trees of *Acer palmatum* clothed in their new red foliage. Bright yellow jewels of yellow gleamed from the kingcups around the pool and the small ground-covering plant *Waldsteinia ternata*. This relative of the potentilla clothes the ground in a dense carpet of strawberry-like trifoliate leaves. In autumn these take on a burnished hue, but in spring new green leaves soon spread among them and subtend abundant bright yellow five-petalled flowers. I introduced a small plant to my garden last year, and it is already spreading pleasingly on poor, shady and rather dry soil, and rooting as it spreads to create an impenetrable weed-proof mat.

Tucked into moist pockets of soil amid rocks were clumps of lemon-yellow *Erythronium* 'Pagoda' and the bright yellowy-green foliage of *Tellima grandiflora*. However, for me the most magical flower was the umbrella plant, *Peltiphyllum peltatum,* as yet unadorned by a single one of its characteristic huge round scallop-edged glossy green leaves. The flowers rear stark against the rocks, and very unlikely they look with thick fleshy tapering white-furred stems some twelve inches tall, topped off with a cluster of pale pink bergenia-like flowers. Even stranger are the thick black snake-like rhizomes which can be seen clinging tightly to the mossy boulders over which the plant has spread.

Slow to establish, sophisticated ground cover was provided by areas of *Epimedium x versicolor*, a member of a genus of plants which rejoice in two dissimilar but evocative common names, barrenwort and bishop's hat. About the former name I can only speculate, but bishop's hat doubtless reflects the attractive elongate heart-shaped leaves which, turned on end, resemble the shape of a mitre. Throughout the seasons these leaves, about one inch long, are a delight, tinted pink or red when young, deeper green and conspicuously veined in summer, and colouring yellow and bronze in autumn. There are a number of species in cultivation with carmine, red, yellow, pink or violet flowers. These flowers are small, and borne dangling on short sprays just reaching above the leaves. *Epimedium x versicolor* has pale yellow flowers, only about a quarter inch across, but intricate in form and slightly reminiscent of a skein of tiny narcissus blooms.

Another plant which greatly took my fancy is not a ground smotherer, for abruptly after flowering it dies down and disappears till next year, leaving other plants the space for summer spreading. This is *Lathyrus vernus*, a member of the pea family, which in April forms dense green clumps, about one foot high and wide, crowned with sprays of blue buds and regal purple pea flowers. The leaflets are bright green and reminiscent of fresh young wisteria foliage. *Lathyrus vernus* is perhaps not the plant for the meticulously tidy gardener, for where it grows young seedlings seem to spring up all over the place, between rocks, in paths, in damp shade or exposed gravel. There are many places in my not-too-tidy garden where it would be welcome, especially where late spreading perennials like rodgersia and brunnera are presently surrounded by bare earth. By June their canopies will be extensive, but by then *Lathyrus vernus*, the spring pea, will have retreated underground in anticipation of the spring to come.

1990

Landscaping a slope

A distinctive feature of gardening in our area is the challenge presented by a sloping landscape. Flat gardens are indeed the exception rather than the rule. Small town gardens are often among the worst, with tiny rear rectangles rising rapidly above the level of the back door. In the country, traditional houses are often built on a minimally sized flat platform carved out of the hillside, with barely space to walk behind the building, or indeed none at all, damp earth pressing directly on the rear wall of pantry and kitchen.

Landscaping slopes is a tricky problem and one requiring not only artistic vision but basic building skills. In view of this it surprises me what scant attention is paid to the sloping garden in many of the attractive books devoted to the principles of garden design. Two components are fundamental: sloping gardens require steps to make them comfortably accessible in all weathers, and most gardeners require at least some areas of horizontal terracing, whether for children's play, ease of cultivation, or to site vital structures like sheds and greenhouses.

Steps and terraces, once created, are likely to become permanent features of the landscape and as such deserve as much serious attention as the appearance of the house. It is sad, therefore, how many otherwise well appointed houses, particularly those built in the first half of this century, have back gardens approached by hideous moulded concrete steps of terrifying steepness, with tall risers and narrow treads so mean that the riser is inclined outwards and upwards to give an extra inch of toehold. Lacking any handrail, prone to iciness in winter, and rising ten or more steps in a single flight, these budget stairways are daunting to the fit and healthy, and must surely take their toll of both the young and the aged.

Aesthetics and comfort both favour a different approach to design. Steps can be most attractive to look upon, and should as far as possible come in short flights of five or six with a landing or terrace on which to draw breath. If shallow in height, say six inches, and with a broad tread of 14–15 inches, they are comfortable to climb, safe in all weathers, and can even be negotiated while trundling a light, large-wheeled garden barrow.

Where steps must rise a great height over a short horizontal distance, it is worth considering a switchback path cut into the slope rather than one direct ascent.

The recent terracing work in my own back garden has tamed a quite modest slope, but none the less demonstrated the importance of competent building skills. Even low retaining walls hold back a very substantial weight of soil and must be built on a firm foundation. Dry-stone walls should have the stones bedded slightly inward, leaning from the horizontal to reduce the risk of slippage and letting rainwater run back into the crevices between the stones. If mortared, or built in block or brick-work, drainage holes are essential.

Wet soil exerts a tremendous force, and every winter a few amateurish garden walls burst spectacularly under its pressure. It has become quite a hobby of mine to look for pipes or weep holes running through the base of soil-retaining walls around the town. Where they are absent, the owner is likely to be sitting on, or beside, a time bomb.

1993

Brynhyfryd escapes the frost

Every gardener with early-flowering rhododendrons and azaleas has watched with delight and disbelief as frost-free nights have followed one upon another and for the first time in several years the exquisite flowers have escaped undamaged.

The delicate young foliage of the Japanese maples has emerged in all its feathery perfection. *Magnolia stellata* flowered unscathed and now the big town trees of *Magnolia soulangeana* are arrayed with their fat candle-like flowers. Even as I write this I worry lest our luck may change and like last year they will all be converted overnight into limp, stained handkerchiefs.

The secluded woodland gardens hidden in the hills are now bejewelled with fresh young growth. Foremost among them is Mrs Dorothy Paish's magical hideaway at Brynhyfryd, Corris, which was formerly a regular member of the National Gardens Scheme's 'Yellow Book'. This year there is a rare opportunity to visit when the garden will be open with the additional attractions of teas and stalls organised

trichotomum, and the tree fern *Dicksonia antarctica*. Students of pruning might seek out Professor Pollock's *Cedrus deodara* on the rock garden by the house. While the one in Joy's arboretum is a stately conical tree, with feathery branches sweeping the ground, his deodar forms a green carpet, its leading shoot removed to promote a quite different habit.

1995

Japanese knotweed: the menace continues

Regular readers may have come, by now, to expect an annual diatribe from me on the subject of Japanese knotweed. However, for this eccentricity I make no apology, for if gardeners have inadvertently contributed a plant of substantial detriment to the ecology, this must surely be it.

Every year the waving plumes of knotweed advance upon roadsides and river banks in Wales and south-west England, and every year precious little is done about it.

Indeed, roadsides of the A487 through Eglwysfach and Derwenlas present a strangely alien appearance in high summer, with verdant thickets of the huge canes, each bearing floppy heart-shaped leaves and a froth of white flowers waving high overhead.

Each year the barren, windswept roadsides of Plynlimon acquire new patches of the plant, which is deceptively hardy despite its luxuriant appearance, and over a few years the sparse spindly canes expand to a dense thicket, banishing the verge-side wildflowers—speedwells, potentillas, milkweeds and hawkbits—for ever.

On that road, I also always gaze in awe at a small cottage set on the hillside above the road near Eisteddfa Gurig. Outside its front windows a small rectangular lawn is laid entirely to Japanese knotweed, by August a surreal eight-foot lawn. I long to learn whether the owner was caught out by buying in topsoil contaminated by root fragments, or whether it is a daring visual joke.

The results of a study of the plant conducted by Richard Moorhead and Laing on behalf of the Welsh Development Agency have now been made public, and are discouraging. Japanese knotweed, although hardly spread except by the hand of man, is here to stay.

It is not believed to set seed in this country, and is disseminated largely by the movement of contaminated topsoil, by earth-moving machines and, perhaps to a lesser extent, by streams and rivers. Never has it been easier to scrape up topsoil and move it around, selling it for landscaping purposes or simply dumping it on wasteground if it is rubbly and unsaleable. The practice of discarding organic garden waste into nearby streams and rivers also remains regrettably widespread. Even small chunks of knotweed rhizome provided only with a single node will rapidly start a new colony in a new situation, and the report concludes that its foothold in the Principality is already so extensive that only containment is considered practicable.

Of course, where knotweed threatens to engulf a multi-million-pound development, a solution is found. The massive roots of the plant, and its new spring shoots like giant asparagus, can break up tarmacadam, but it will yield to a series of applications of Glyphosate, (Tumbleweed or Greenscape to the gardener, Roundup in farmers' terminology).

At local level gardeners have won victories. At Bryneithin Hall, Llanfarian, a mighty clump, encroaching from among the bamboos to engulf the sweeping lawns, was destroyed by applications of hydrated lime (it is an acid-loving plant), by burying and digging. Other gardeners reach annually for the Glyphosate, diluting it with an added squirt of washing up liquid for better plant-wetting abilities. Organic gardeners will dig and burn the roots and rhizomes. On no account send this rampant opportunist via the dustbin to your local dump!

But what about our riversides, some now impassible in a jungle of giant peashooters? And our exquisitely diverse verges and hedgerows? Will the residents of Derwenlas and Eglwysfach put pressure on their district councillors and demand an eradication programme? Or will these village sink silently into a sea of the alien weed?

1991

Dolwen, Llanrhaeadr-ym-Mochnant

Mary Wesley's heroines invariably have three talents in the department of middle-class female excellence—cooking, gardening and sex. Readers of her novels will be aware how skilfully these three elements of accomplishment are interwoven; sometimes the one is a form of gainful employment, sometimes another, but in later life her heroines are serene, content and possess marvellous gardens. These stories owe their appeal to two messages: that sex was invented long before the sixties, and that though one may retire gracefully from the sex, the gardening goes on for ever.

Frances Denby might have stepped straight from the pages of a Wesley novel, as she stands in the drizzle to welcome a bus load of visitors from the Cardiganshire Horticultural Society. It was a very small, golden-coloured bus, rented out by Dyfed County Council and rather exaggeratedly styling itself 'Executive'. We had been (correctly) advised that a larger coach would not negotiate the intricate lanes leading to her home. In excruciating discomfort we descended like twenty-three broilers granted our freedom. Mrs Denby's home is in Clwyd, a mile outside the village of Llanrhaeadr-ym-Mochnant and approached up one of those high-banked lanes admitting only the narrowest of vehicles and totally devoid of passing places. Here stood the epitome of older gardeners' chic, the sensible trousering, dusty pink Oxford shirting, harmonizing handwoven waistcoat, topped off by a thick felt underfelt-coloured sou'wester. What amateurs we felt, fiddling with our anoraks and umbrellas.

Frances Denby is a a real gardener. She drew no plans but allowed the landscape to tell her what to do with it. It is clear that it is still making suggestions to her, for as one strays farther from the old cottage one reaches a succession of three ponds, each one younger than the one before, the third only recently planted with marginals and choice shrubs. Every plant she grows is burgeoning with health. Good gardening is ruthless—if it doesn't thrive it goes. A garden in her philosophy is a place for happy plants; it has no place for hospital cases.

Also she allows the garden to speak for itself, and most eloquently it does so. Visitors are invited to scatter and discover the landscape. Silently it exhibits good plantsmanship, rich mulching, weed-free borders, and all the plant names one could wish for, each hand-painted in white upon a little fragment of slate beside the plant. Garden ornament can be a sensitive issue. I could name gardens suddenly convulsed by an entirely inappropriate Japanese lantern, a plastic urn or a plaster donkey. Frances Denby's ornaments are bronze, not too numerous, and appropriately placed. There is a stylized cat sharpening its claws on the laburnum, a gardening figure in a hat almost as characterful as Mrs Denby's, which rests its foot upon a spade, a hawk just alighting on a strategically placed pinnacle of rock beside the pool.

Frances Denby and her partner came here twenty years ago. Surrounded by the spectacular scenery of the Berwyn mountains, and just down the lane from one of Wales's picturesque highlights, the 240-foot Pistyll Rhaeadr, they barely felt the need for a garden. But following his death and the opportunity to purchase four and a half acres of adjoining farmland, the garden began to expand. Now she is in a position to make it pay its keep.

Open to the public on Fridays and the last Sunday in the month in aid of the National Gardens Scheme and local charities, she also hosts groups and a garden school run on certain weeks in summer. Here another Wesley skill is paramount: the catering is excellent, and who needs to be taught how to garden when they can learn by example how to grow old gracefully?

1995

june

Wildflower gardening at Winllan

As wild flowers have increasingly disappeared from Britain's fields and hedgerows, public interest has turned to wildflower gardening, and few seed merchants have omitted a wildflower 'series' for the small gardener and ready-made mixtures for seeding a wildflower meadow or lawn. Sadly too many packets of such seed end up scattered in the poorest and wildest areas of our gardens where they will readily fail in competition with larger, ranker weeds.

Long-standing exponents of the skills of wildflower gardening are Ian and Katharyn Callan of Winllan, Talsarn, eight miles north of Lampeter, who open their garden to the public in aid of the National Gardens Scheme.

Six acres of land sloping gently south to the bank of the Aeron river have been converted, over the years, from an ordinary pasture to an amazingly diverse wildflower meadow, a patch of native woodland, and a lovely riverside walk where as many as eleven species of dragonflies and damselflies have been recorded. There is a good chance of glimpsing the iridescent plumage of the resident kingfishers or the precise movements and striking black and white plumage of the several pied flycatchers which breed in nest boxes in the garden.

All this has been achieved, interestingly, without recourse to the seed packet, but simply by creating the right conditions to favour a varied flora of local plants. The meadow, now speckled with the colours of ragged robin, eyebright, hay rattle, buttercups and milkwort, is never sprayed with selective herbicides, nor cropped for hay before the seeds have set. In these conditions a wide variety of meadow wildflowers flourish, and six kinds of orchids, notoriously impossible to uproot and transplant, have spontaneously reappeared, presumably from roots long present in the meadow but, under usual methods of pasture management, too disadvantaged ever to bloom.

The long dormancy of seed awaiting an appropriate opportunity was emphasized by the Callans' experience with a dry bank descending to the meadow and formerly choked in bracken, bramble, gorse and willow. Scraped completely bare by a mechanical digger, the land was not reseeded, yet within two years it was awash with ox-eye daisies, violets, cat's-ear and cowslip appearing, as it were, from nowhere.

Ian Callan is keen to point out the distinction between a wildlife garden and a garden allowed to run wild. The former requires active management, and regular attacks on the thistle, plantain and bracken which will all too readily take over unless checked. Fertilizers, too, although welcomed in moderation by many plants, can be a danger to the plant community through unduly favouring larger grasses like rye grass, cocksfoot and timothy.

Traditional gardening skills are also very much in evidence in the form of the extensive, beautifully tended lawn which slopes from the house to the very attractive landscaped pond flanked by native bog plants (and inhabited by leeches) in which conservation guru David Bellamy was recently pictured swimming with the owner. There are also fruit trees, shrub borders and herbaceous beds which adjoin the house.

1991

Fish, flesh and fowl at the Chelsea Flower Show

Garden sculpture—was there ever a greater pitfall to avoid? Plants are easy by comparison, their lines flow, their colours need follow only a few simple rules to harmonize and delight. Garden pots are pretty straightforward, too, and generally enhance the whole. But though many designers favour a representational sculpture, the gardens at the Chelsea Flower Show exhibited little that was innovative and striking, and much that could have been better sited or left out. Leaping fish in Askham Bryan's Garden of Hope seemed static and too bulky, quite out of scale with the tiny cascade which was their setting. The imagination soon placed them gasping and moribund upon the streamlet's margin or slithering, bruised, ignominious, down the cascade. There was an epidemic of deer, plonked here and there, one in the Garden of Hope, another beside the *Daily Mirror*'s woodland pool, and a particularly nasty duo of Stag and Doe caught immobile among the golden conifers of the Yardley/*Daily Express* Garden of Natural Beauty. Designers should think more about scale when siting naturalistic statues: the Shellseeker, a nice little child model by Vanessa Marsden in the foreground of the Preferred Direct/*House Beautiful* garden was just too small for the plants she squatted among: she should have been larger, or younger, for the eye not to be drawn to this disharmony.

A refreshing exception was the Brussel Sprout fountain by Simon Allison in the *Country Living* garden. A commissioned piece, this was inspirational, realistic, appropriate to the theme of decorative vegetables, and above all, to scale. Worked in bronze, it will not be cheap.

It is in the field of garden ceramics that new, quirky and inexpensive designers are to be found. High-fired stoneware becomes impermeable to water and is entirely frost-resistant, yet according to the finish and glaze employed, ceramics will grow lichens and mosses like sculpted stone, or remain smooth and with the patina of beaten metal. A particularly exiting new designer on this scene is Dennis Fairweather of Hillside House, Starston, Harleston, Norfolk, exhibiting for the first time at Chelsea this year. Three of his distinctive abstract shapes, radially grooved and suggestive of the shapes of sea urchin, had been selected by designer Fiona Lawrensen for the PD/*House Beautiful* garden. Drilled, they had been adapted as peacefully upwelling fountains.

The future for Dennis Fairweather deserves to lie with his humorous and representational pieces. Chunkily appealing guinea fowl and bantams with feathered feet cried out, nay squawked, to be casually grouped in the garden, perhaps changing their location from time to time—now under bushes in the heat, another day clustered by the pool. Penguins, owls, ducks, geese and other more fanciful birds similarly invite imaginative siting. There is many a green courtyard garden which would be improved, not by another granite Japanese lantern, dry bird bath or sunless sundial, but by one of Fairweather's planted heads. Primitive Easter Island style heads wear a fine upstanding head of blue oat grass hair (*Helictotrichon sempervirens*), while 'Major Planter' is a rather superior moustachioed bust whose luxuriant head is adorned with green curls of sempervivum. And many a waterbutt would be enlivened by one of Fairweather's amiable water gargoyles, whose hands grasp the rim of the barrel while the emergent face emits a steady stream of water from its pursed lips.

Ceramic sculptures are originals, because they are handbuilt, durable, and yet, on account of their clay material, cheap compared with other sculpture. Fairweather's prices range from £65 to £450. Here I found a new, humorous, and very British voice, a welcome change from all that sober classicism, and the discordant orientalism too prevalent in the garden.

1995

A first visit to Carrog

One of the high points of the local gardener's summer is the open day at Carrog, Llandeiniol, a small, Georgian 'Gentleman's Residence', now home of Geoffrey and Maureen Williams. It is an opportunity to meet unusual plants and familiar gardeners, the latter looking wistfully at the former. As I have come to expect, their chosen date was favoured with pleasant weather and an excellent tea on the lawns.

The garden is five acres in extent, much of it created by Mr and Mrs Williams among the mature oaks of pre-existing woodland sheltered from the westerly winds in the lee of a long spur of hill. Meandering lawned walks take one down the hillside through diverse shrubs and trees to a natural pond with golden carp and wires stretched across the surface to deter the herons. After skirting the pond, beside the vast prickly-stemmed leaves of *Gunnera manicata*, handsome stands of *Primula japonica* and huge spiky clubs of the skunk cabbage *Lysichiton americanus*, one climbs the slope again to enter the ordered world of an old walled garden. Here one finds a tidy vegetable patch with soft fruit enclosed in netting, a formal pond beside an exquisite golden full moon maple *Acer japonicum aureum*, and a lean-to greenhouse populated by insectivorous plants, some of them exotically in bloom.

It is, though, the trees and shrubs which strike deepest envy in the visiting gardeners. Most spectacular this year was *Styrax japonica*, an exquisitely shaped tree fifteen to twenty feet tall, which bears masses of small white golden-centred flowers pendent beneath narrow oval green leaves. This is the perfect tree under which to sit or lie on a summer day, looking up to a ceiling of flowers. Also in the walled garden were several shrubs often considered tender in our climate: *Crinodendron hookerianum,* the Chilean lantern tree, with its red fleshy dangling lantern flowers beneath the branches, *Eccremocarpus scaber* and *Tropaeolum speciosum* clambering over other shrubs, and against the walls the strangely magical-looking red and yellow blooms of *Abutilon megapotamicum*.

Outside the walled garden, but benefiting from the wall's protection, were *Solanum crispum,* the Chilean potato tree, a shrub covered, as its name implies, with blue and gold potato flowers, and another enthusiasts' tree from Chile, *Embothrium coccineum lanceolatum* flowering in fluffy flames of red.

It is difficult to single out favourites in so large a garden, for the woodland contains many delights. Among the flowering shrubs, I particularly liked the blue-tinged foliage and sharp pink briar blooms of *Rosa rubrifolia,* and the delicately scented pink flowers of *Kolkwitzia amabilis.* The owners are conscientious with their labelling, especially of the larger trees, and among the native oaks one finds *Quercus coccinea,* an oak with large soft leaves and bark like wild-silk wallpaper; *Betula albosinensis septentrionalis,* a birch with copper-pink peeling bark; *Sorbus aria* 'Mitchellii', a particularly handsome whitebeam, and *Ulmus carpinifolia sarniensis aurea,* a shapely narrow conical golden-leaved elm. My only regret is that the garden is not open at rhododendron-time, autumn colour time and all the other stages of the year, each doubtless a fresh delight.

1989

Llanllyr opens its doors

Many gardeners will be tempted once more to abandon the weeding this Sunday afternoon in favour of a visit to Llanllyr, Talsarn, home of Robert and Loveday Gee, which opens to the public in support of the National Gardens Scheme, and St Hilary's Church Fund, Trefilan.

Llanllyr opened its gates to gardeners in 1991, displaying a host of innovative designs and plantings instituted since Mrs Gee took the garden seriously in hand in 1986. Now approaching nine years' maturity, the impact of the new features is fully apparent. New yew hedges are, of course, particularly slow growing and still in their infancy, but it is a heart-warming feature of this garden that formal designs likely to be improved by 100 years or more of management have been confidently entered upon in the 1980s.

Perhaps the confidence is born of history—Llanllyr has been in the hands of Mrs Gee's family, the Leweses for 200 years. Until recently a rather gaunt and dilapidated large house overlooking the Aeron river on the B4337 Llanrhystud to Lampeter road, in the last decade it has been trimly restored, rendered in browny cream, and the garden extended and manicured where neglected Victorian shrubbery and pasture previously lay. For every aspiring plantsman it is a pleasure to stroll the lawns and scrutinize the borders around the house. Mrs Gee is a knowledgeable and enthusiastic plant collector who often purchases new plants and varieties at major flower shows. Since plants on sale at the open day are mainly surplus material propagated from the garden itself, there is the opportunity to acquire some choice plants, having first seen them in a garden setting.

A major element of the new garden is the long rose border which runs alongside the whitewashed mud wall of the kitchen garden. To a design by Hazel le Rougetel, the roses are planted in groups so that their colour grades from white, through apricot and pale pink, to darker pinks and eventually red. At a cross path the sequence halts and is planted again, in mirror image beyond the central point. Challenging the old idea that roses should have nothing but manure at their feet, here a contrasting under-carpet has been devised, with acid green foliage beneath the white roses, bronze under the apricot, glaucous beneath the light pink, silver beneath the dark pink, and blue and purple flowers beneath the red.

Adjoining the end of the rose border a niche in the wall shelters an inscribed early Christian monument. Split down its axis long ago, perhaps by builders in need of a good lintel, the surviving half displays part of a cross and the inscribed title to a gift of land.

Another innovation runs parallel to the rose garden, a narrow canal-form water garden spanned by a delightful cobbled low hump bridge, and fed by a small cascade from a stone lion's mouth. Sinuous retaining walls flank the grass-bordered canal and the young yews are now linking up to enclose the whole in a long narrow corrider of beetling perspective. One can readily imagine the bulk and impact of these assured lines after a century of clipping has created impenetrable living walls.

1993

The colour wheel in the garden

When my husband elected to attract attention by wearing a yellow shirt with lilac cummerbund and tie, the comments received did not, on the whole, commend the tastefulness of the ensemble. However, in the field of gardening, this colour scheme would win the undoubted seal of approval from arbiters of style as influential as Rosemary Verey, gardener, writer, and broadcaster, who recently addressed the Cardiganshire Horticultural Society in Aberystwyth.

Mrs Verey dwelt in some detail upon the exquisite complementary plantings at Barnsley House, Gloucestershire, of tall purple alliums beneath a long laburnum arch trailing yellow racemes of bloom. Other combinations included *Buddleia alternifolia*, whose weeping branches wear regular clusters of mauve, as a cascading background to yellow iris and pinky-mauve polygonum, or the greeny-yellow heads of *Euphorbia characias* jostling with purple-blooming *Erysimum* 'Bowles' Mauve' or hardy geraniums.

In my own garden I favour the handsome, if malodorous, yellow *Iris pyrenaicum* beside *Thalictrum delavayi* 'Hewitt's Double' and the tall sculptured columns of purple lupins.

Such a colour combination is described as a complementary pair, as she illustrated on the colour wheel which is segmentally arranged to display red opposite green, orange opposite blue, and yellow opposite violet. Having nothing of hue in common they enhance one another by extreme contrast, a situation more reliably tasteful in plants, it appears, than in evening wear!

Harmony, meanwhile, can be guaranteed where adjoining colours on the wheel and varying shades are skilfully combined.

Such rules are useful, but there is probably no colour combination which cannot work, especially where colour is just one facet of a composition of foliage and flowers. However, extra caution is called for where flowering is so spectacular as to totally submerge the greenery. On a visit to Colby Woodland Garden near Tenby, we found that even National Trust gardeners are not innocent of some unfortunate juxtapositions. Among the more recent plantings, the eye reeled at brilliant red rhododendron blooms clashing horribly with adjoining cerise, and wearied at a random cluster of deciduous azaleas forming together all the impact of a nest of pastel paper handkerchiefs.

Nearer home is a gateway where new plantings of deciduous azaleas have been put in as a foreground to huge purple *Rhododendron ponticum* shrubs and a strong pink *Rhododendron arboreum*. When these burst, recently, into bloom, they proved to be a most discordant choice, tomato-soup red, and salmon-paste beige, charming in themselves but deadened in their context. Fortunately azaleas are shallow-rooted and readily transplanted, so perhaps next season they will have been moved to a more harmonious neighbourhood.

1993

Tea and taxidermy

It is not always the flowers which make the deepest impression on a garden visit. At Acton Round Hall in Shropshire it was almost everything but. First of all it was not a round hall, rather a fine rectangular Georgian brick house built in 1715 for Sir Whitmore Acton, of Aldenham. Owing to a superfluity of family seats, he had barely moved in before he moved out again, back to Aldenham, and Acton Round Hall stood empty on the family acres for the next two hundred years. During this time the locust tree, *Robinia pseudoacacia,* in front of the house grew to prodigious size, serendipitously obscuring the twentieth-century view towards Dudley and the Merrifield Shopping Centre.

The Hall finally came into usage in the present century and acquired a few 1930s garden features along the way. Our initial impressions were of a conventional English garden, with broad borders, yew hedges and meandering lawns, drifts of catmint underplanting the roses. We did find the follies a little bizarre. Mrs Kennedy, who has lived here since 1971, explained that they were a hobby of her husband's. Nearest the house was a charming little Gothic summerhouse, constructed with reclaimed architectural components from Wolverhampton. The skyline beyond was broken by the castellation which had been added to a pretty ordinary breeze block barn. The pagoda had been his response to her reasonable request for a potting shed. There had been a little difficulty with planning permission for the pagoda, three storeys tall, with roofs of corrugated plastic, but the Kennedys had prevailed. Not far away, Scruffy the faithful terrier lay interred beneath a handsome obelisk of stone. Her epitaph pulled no punches:

Severe incontinence cut short
A long life at the age of
18 years
June 21 1985
If her bladder had been stronger
She would have lasted even longer

I was among the last of the Cardiganshire Horticultural Society group to push open the front door as invited, and come in for tea. I suppose I expected chintzy sofas, copies of *Country Life*, family portraits. Instead I found myself facing a huge stuffed lion, his face frozen in mid-roar. Behind him the entire wall was lined with African weapons of stabbing, slashing and cutting. Above my head a male baboon squatted, free arm outstretched, on the central chandelier. On the side tables were two monkeys' torsos, one clasping his forehead in thought, the other balanced on his forelimbs alone, under a glass dome.

I was there for the tea, and the tea was truly excellent. Crisp-edged fresh-baked scones, tiny homemade cream meringues, gâteau, fruit cake and more. But the Victoria Jubilee marquetry table where I balanced my teacup was a little unusual. It stood on four legs, real ones with hooves: the feet and ankles of a giraffe. Another of Mr Hew Kennedy's hobbies is big game and many of the trophies are, or were, personal acquaintances. Mrs Kennedy took me through into the hallway to see the giraffe's tail, hanging like a bell pull, beside the tail of an elephant whose feet stood nearby. Each tail was capped on the stump by a little copper plate.

The stair wall bore a traditional display of trophy heads, many of them antique, but they dimmed beside the immediacy of the modern taxidermist's art. On the half landing a buck sable antelope stepped out from the curtains, his hooves upon a white cushion. At least, the front half of him did; perhaps the rear was in another room. It seems rude to explore too far into another person's home, but I can report that the giraffe's head, and some six feet of its neck, stood on its stump on the upstairs landing.

The largest canvas on the wall was a bird picture, which depicted a white pelican, spreadeagled with its bag beak dangling open, a very dead roller in the bottom corner, and sundry other elements of the sporting bag. A little fatigued I instead let my eyes rest on a bright sunny scene of a square in Rome. There were lots of people in the picture, in ones, twos and larger groups. One seemed to be looking down a well. Only when I stepped closer did I fully appreciate I was admiring a sixteenth-century representation of the Massacre of the Senate in Rome, a greater serving of decapitation and disembowelment than I usually take with my tea.

1996

The ethical nightmare of the garden seat

There was a time when shopping for garden furniture was governed by purely personal and practical considerations of style, comfort and cost. Balancing the three, richer gardeners might be expected to select a handsome hardwood bench, poorer ones a rustic softwood seat tacked together with galvanized nails, or a recreational-area-style picnic table.

No longer is life so simple. Gardeners are, on the whole, ecologically aware and concerned about the degradation of the environment. These days, buying garden furniture is an ethical nightmare which could leave many of us sitting on the ground, as we wrestle with the rival claims upon our consciences.

First stop on my shopping route was Arthur Newman's garden centre, where I found two ranges of very attractive hardwood furniture. Both had nostalgic motifs, fitting complements to the widespread Gertrude Jekyll nostalgia which pervades garden design. Swan-Hattersley of Telford's 'Rushbury' bench (five feet long and costing £369) particularly caught my eye with its Victorian-Gothic-style ogee slatting of the seat-back. These seats are largely constructed with traditional mortice and tenon joints, though the principal components are then bolted together when you receive the flat pack.

A comparable range is made by Bridgeman Leisure of Enfield, Middlesex and sold fully assembled. Benches are embossed on the back rail with Arts-and-Crafts designs of flowers, wheat or acorns. A modest £139 buys a basic four-foot bench of modern appearance while £249 buys a handsome seat with broad arms and an oak leaf and acorn motif.

Here lies the moral dilemma. These acorns never saw an oak tree, they decorate Ghanaian iroko, an extremely competitively priced and durable hardwood which will resist decay for twenty-five years of garden service. Both Bridgeman and Swan-Hattersley furniture come festooned with a rich literature of self-justification about proper forest management, sustained yield programmes and supporting Third-World economics.

Real oak is an expensive hardwood which weathers silvery and lasts well in outdoor use. Pren Welsh Oak, of Blaenpennal, Aberystwyth, offered a display at the recent Aberystwyth Show, and purchasers can be confident that their seat will derive from and contribute to the effective management of local woodlands. A handsome traditional (but not particularly comfortable) five-foot bench, 'The Hafod', costs £546, substantially more than even the 'Rushbury'. Comfortable and more affordable was the less elegant 'Ystwyth' bench, 52 inches long and costing only £176.

Principles do not necessarily come cheap, but another solution is to buy rustic larch pole furniture, grown and assembled locally. Mid-Wales Rustic Furniture of Llandrindod Wells might snag your clothing and will require annual treatment with preservative, but at £70 for a three-seater bench, or £85 for one with a built-in table and parasol hole, it is rugged, practical and costs little more than the family groceries.

Cheaper still, and quite adequate to support two behinds, is the

Allibert white plastic dove seat at £46. This will, of course, bowl around the garden in high winds. While neither endangering tropical hardwoods nor supporting Third-World regimes, the purchaser still has pollution by the petrochemical industry upon his conscience.

1993

july

Number 7 Maes yr Awel started life as a Terrapin bungalow, portable housing put up to accommodate the engineers working on Nant y Moch reservoir. Some of its neighbours were indeed folded up and taken elsewhere, and as time passed the present housing estate of council homes and old people's bungalows brought services and communal clipped grass to the development.

Mrs Birch's temporary house, meanwhile, took deeper and deeper root, extending in various directions with kitchen and conservatory, and the garden began, haltingly, to take shape among the mature birch trees on the hillside. Pausing regularly at Percy Thrower's Garden Centre on trips to the Midlands, she bought ornamental conifers, roses, herbaceous plants and thus began a personal investigation of the range of plants tolerant of thin acid soil, wind and altitude.

Hybrid tea roses do not, on the whole, like this situation, but Mrs Birch grows 'Albertine' over a pergola and has found an exquisite soft pink floribunda-type rose which loves it here and wears a cascade of blossom above shiny bright green leaves from now until September.

Junipers, prostrate and erect, golden, blue and green, flourish, as do many different varieties of cupressus, yew and holly. Colour is provided by *Spiraea japonica* 'Little Princess', *Potentilla fruticosa* in many shades, and quite a variety of hardy geraniums. Summer bedding plants, in borders and containers add to the array, and you may find some recent introductions like the magically fragrant chocolate plant, *Cosmos atrosanguineus,* in an urn near the house.

The garden paths lead one to a series of enclosed spaces, with pools, fountains, small lawns and patios. Living walls of clipped trees form the boundaries. It is perhaps in the range of carefully trimmed evergreens that this garden has most to teach us. In a confined garden many of Beryl's purchases could have got thoroughly out of hand were it not for regular trimming. Structure and topiary is largely the work of her partner Nick Stead, and includes a multi-hued flat-topped hedge in variegated holly, a Christmas tree fashioned like a flat-topped circular coffee table, arches of yew, deodar and hawthorn. Anyone with a loose-textured undisciplined Leylandii hedge should pay homage here. Regular clipping has produced a wall which is dense, green and as solid to lean on as a carthorse.

1993

So at last my rose has found an identity and perhaps a few more admirers. I have yet, though, to find 'Maria Liesa' in a British rose catalogue. Her admirers (if any) would probably need to start with a cutting: a ripe shoot just past flowering should be suitable. As a general rule it is claimed the closer a rose is to its wild ancestors, the more readily it strikes root. With this venerable Frau it should be easy.

1991

Meg Merilees and the American Pillar

My article last year on the subject of my vigorous shocking-pink old-fashioned rambler rose generated a shower of correspondence from rose enthusiasts. What it did not create was a clear consensus on my rose's name, for as my informants on the subject of the now unfashionable 'American Pillar' rose multiplied, so also did the roses they described.

In Peter Beales's authoritative volume *Classic Roses*, 'American Pillar' is described as having simple flowers, at first reddish pink, paling to deep pink with white centres. David Austin, however, another respected rose grower, offers a carmine rambler without a white eye under the same name. Mr J. J. Richards of Pontrhydfendigaid described his 'American Pillar' as light pink darkening to medium pink and developing a beautiful perfume before petal fall. My rose has barely any scent and never drops its petals; they shrivel and brown on the spray and are soon concealed by subsequently opened flowers.

As the plot thickened the flowering season waned, so this year I set off promptly to the garden of Mr and Mrs Sherrington of Tynygraig, Ystrad Meurig, a truss of my own rose blossom in one hand. Mr Sherrington's 'American Pillar' had an established lineage: it was brought as a cutting from an old plant near Bridport in Dorset.

I was greatly relieved to find it closely resembled my rose, and author Peter Beales's description. The vigorous arching canes bear side branches decked with flowers, up to fifty buds to a truss, giving a prolonged period of flowering. The leaves are large and glossy green, composed of at least seven and often nine leaflets. The wide-open five-petalled flower displays a large boss of yellow stamens, which later shrivel and incurve, making the white eye more conspicuous. Most remarkable of all is the petal retention. Like the double blooms of 'Albertine', the flowers remain for well over a week, paling, shrivelling and turning brown on the plant.

My confusion was further reduced when Mr Sherrington showed me another rambler, at first glance indistinguishable from 'American Pillar', which is named 'Meg Merilees'. The same colour, the same white eye on flowers borne in large clusters, but beneath this pergola was a carpet of freshly dropped heart-shaped pink petals. Other distinctions also became apparent: 'Meg Merilees' is very spiny, armoured right up the flower stem with numerous ferocious tiny spines. The young receptacle is prone to powdery mildew, the leaves are smaller, un-glossy and composed of just five serrated leaflets; the flowers often have an extra petal or two (typically seven) and an exquisite scent.

'Meg Merilees', I learn, is a Hybrid Sweetbriar, an older rose raised from *Rosa eglanteria* on the estates of Lord Penzance at the end of the nineteenth century. She is thus senior to 'American Pillar' (1909), which is a Wichuraiana Hybrid, created in the early years of this century, and probably indistinguishable from the East German cultivar 'Maria Liesa'. Unlike the sweetbriars, these newer roses offer no autumn display, for they set no fruit.

1992

Footnote: In David Austin's *Shrub and Climbing Roses* (Antique Collectors Club 1993) he describes American Pillar as a Wichuraiana Hybrid *with* a white eye.

An unnamed rose at Ystrad Meurig

My recent visit to Mr and Mrs Sherrington's garden at Tynygraig, Ystrad Meurig, did more than sort out the mystery of 'Meg Merilees' and the 'American Pillar' rose.

As I approached the gate I stopped to gaze in amazement at a white flowering shrub, billowing out beside the gateposts, a mass of white conical sprays of flowers reminiscent of *Hydrangea paniculata*. Hydrangea it was not, and closer inspection revealed a totally unfamiliar, almost thornless rose.

Mr Sherrington reacted with no surprise when I exclaimed I had never seen anything like it. He had bred it himself, by self-pollinating a miniature rose which showed a tendency to largeness. The result, unnamed and not revealed to august bodies such as the Rose Society, is known within the family as 'Sherry', and is a fine example of the creative possibilities open to all gardeners.

Once invented, it has been propagated by cuttings and has become the signature of this charming garden. It is planted everywhere, forming a loose hedge inside the field hedgerow which makes the boundary; it scrambles over waist-high post-and-rail pathside fencing, and arches up to cast a froth of white blossom eight to ten feet high over evergreen shrubs.

The leaves are long, soft and lightish green, the individual leaflets obovate in shape and well spaced along the central petiole. This year's shoots, each about twelve inches long, are clothed in well-spaced alternate leaves and each topped with an extensive cluster of tiny flowers, on small stems spirally arranged. A good shoot bears as many as a hundred buds and flowers. Tight buds and newly opened blooms have a hint of pink, while the fully open flowers are flat, pure white, five-petalled discs, each a mere half-inch across and exhibiting a handsome golden cluster of stamens.

I found this a ravishing rose especially suitable for an informal, slightly wild, country garden. To be able to brush past it without threat was a treat indeed, for apart from the large pink-flowered Bourbon rose 'Zéphirine Drouhin', there are few thornless roses.

There were many other delights in this plantsman's garden, but the dominant memory is of swags of white rose blossom, humming with bees, billowing on every side.

1992

The Victorian Arboretum at Trawsgoed

The annual Trawsgoed Garden Party afforded a rare opportunity to slip away from the stalls and the teas, the sack race, skittles and the silver band, to look around the grounds of Trawsgoed Mansion, ancestral seat of the Earls of Lisburne, presently in the care of the Welsh Office Agriculture Department.

The garden deserves to be better known, for it has great charm, combining formal and parkland features, and including what is probably the finest arboretum in our area. An avenue of limes flanks the motor approach to the house, while a handsome stand of great oaks leads away in the direction of Llanafan.

The main reception rooms and library look out over a lawn with formal circular pool and fountain, and to one side there is an attractive rockery and series of informal pools fed by a cascading streamlet. Beyond the lawn one descends a series of stepped terraces, passing a small formal rose garden and a statue of the infant Pan, and enters a long straight avenue of monkey puzzles which leads to a handsome semi-circular carved stone seat wrapped around the base of a huge hiba (*Thujopsis dolabrata*).

From here one wanders off through a fine little arboretum, laid out with particular love for cypresses, thujas, rhododendrons and unusual beeches. Planting dates in the main from the late-nineteenth century and some of the trees still retain their embossed metal labels.

All but the experts soon become bewildered by the variety of ornamental cypresses and false cypresses with their strange little rounded cones and their smooth, scaly fronds. However, one emerges with some lasting impressions of the sombre drooping foliage of the Nootka cypress, the feathery textured Arizona cypress, the tall majesty of the wellingtonias and of the extraordinary looming presence of the hiba, whose U-shaped branches descend till they reach the ground so that the tree squats on its elbows in the forest.

The shelter of the many conifers protects perfect specimens of two extraordinary varieties of beech, a weeping form whose thin branches dangle some fifty feet from the crown to trail on the ground, and the fern-leaved beech whose delicate cut leaves form a light but even canopy at many levels, even the trunk and major branches bearing little fern-like tufts of leaves like seaweed on a wreck.

Among the trees are rhododendrons and azaleas, once a very fine collection but now showing the legginess and over-crowding of great age. Guided by Nancy Kirk, whose own lovely rhododendron collection at Llanafan derives in large part from seeds and layered cuttings taken from Trawsgoed in the 1960s, we sought and found old friends and mourned the loss of others, especially of many of the small-flowered, honeysuckle-scented not-so-showy azaleas.

Many local people feel that the contract gardeners who now perform the bulk of Trawsgoed's gardening lack the commitment to its long-term needs which this garden deserves. In time for the fête, bedding plants had been hastily put in and much of the grass rough-cut for the first time this season. Also worrying is the limited evidence of appropriate planting of shrubs or trees for the future.

The garden is a gem, but one which is becoming post-mature, and there is little to be seen which will replace the ageing giants as they die.

1990

Footnote: In 1995 WOAD left Trawsgoed, and it has been re-acquired by the Lisburne family. The detailed plans for the future of the house and garden are not yet known.

The Neuadd garden, Rhaeadr

On a sunny afternoon a friend and I pottered over the hills to Rhaeadr to visit The Neuadd, a substantial manor house set off the B4518 Elan Valley road and noted, in the early past of this century, for its terraces and topiary in Edwardian style.

The Neuadd is now the home of David Wheeler and Simon Dorrell who together launched the magazine *Hortus* into the gardening world in 1987. Modestly describing itself as 'the most intelligent gardening magazine in the world', *Hortus* is a discreet quarterly journal printed on thick cream-coloured paper and illustrated only in black and white—old photographs, engravings and line drawings, many by Simon Dorrell.

Articles are largely by illustrious names from the gardening world, and there is a regular commitment to literature with the Gardens in Fiction series which inspects the works of Jane Austen, Henry James, Virgina Woolf, E. F. Benson and others for their horticultural insights. This spring *Hortus* was joined by a sister magazine, *Convivium*, similar in style and appearance but dedicated to the topic of good eating, and of course to Food in Fiction by a similar galaxy of authors.

Working from home as they do, David Wheeler, Editor and Simon Dorrell, Art Editor, can unwind and muse upon their next publication while re-inventing the four-acre garden which surrounds the house. Clearance and restoration of the long-neglected terraces and rockery are accompanied by the creation of a series of separate gardens or 'garden rooms', each designed to be experienced in isolation from its neighbours and screened from the next by ornamentally clipped hedging of yew and box.

Perhaps our most immediate impression of the new gardens was of an inordinate fondness for columns, urns and obelisks—'Clough-ing it up', as Simon deprecatingly alluded to the influence of Portmeirion architect Clough Williams Ellis upon his thinking.

On arrival at the house one approaches the front door through a spacious barrier of six fifteen-foot columns each painted ochre and topped by a stone cherub bearing mandolin or flute. Below the house, and framed somewhat unexpectedly by the backdrop of the valley, stand four further pedestalled cherubs which in due course will hover on their plinths above sixteen tall dark fastigate yews, each clipped and flat-topped to resemble Italian cypresses. The whole will be enclosed by a rectangular yew hedge, clipped in a Dutch gable design.

Nearby is a sunken herb garden ornamented geometrically with eight obelisks of varying design, and the beginnings of a white garden in a lozenge-shaped enclosure. Another room is to be enclosed at head height by pleached hornbeams and frames a rectangular bed of damp-loving *Iris sibirica* around red terracotta urns.

In the context of all this formality it was a surprise to hear, not the wooden clunk of croquet and the chink of champagne glasses, but the hippy tinklings of modern tubular wind chimes suspended in the old apple trees below the house.

1993

Lisa Raw-Rees dries flowers

Some people have a house and a garden, others have the talent to weld the two together into an inviting living space in which a sense of the garden is ever-present, rain or shine.

Such a gardener is Lisa Raw-Rees whose terraced harbourside home, Moldavia, and adjoining guest-house in Aberaeron, provides a gradual transition from indoors to the garden. The houses, one pink and one red, look much like their neighbours from the front, facing northwards over the harbour, adorned with lush windowboxes of pot dahlias, lobelia and begonias. However, on passing into the house one finds stencilled walls, great informal armfuls of dried flowers, and a long bright conservatory which, running along the rear of the house, extends the cheerful tiled-floored kitchen out towards the patio and small back garden.

The dried flowers are everywhere, hanging in bunches from the ceiling in the guests' breakfast room, dangling like a half-drawn blind from the kitchen curtain rail, thrust in big colourful handfuls into baskets and lying in bunches on the cupboard tops. It comes as a surprise that so much can come from a modest-sized garden without denuding it of flowers. Lisa is an experimental flower drier rather than one who slavishly follows the rules. She dries everything simply by hanging it upside down in air, and the timing of her harvest is determined not by the pundits but by when she feels the flower spike has already served good value in the garden. The huge rich blue spikes of delphiniums are not cut until they have opened all but the final two buds. Having served ten days or so in the border, they pass to immortality indoors.

In addition to the sculptural delphiniums, Lisa dries curry plant, lavender, *Alchemilla mollis, Achillea, Gypsophila*, cornflower and ice-plant harvested in bloom. To my surprise she is equally successful with wild buttercups, which obligingly retain their petals and their colour for years. For the form of their seed heads she dries poppies, *Eryngium, Sidalcea, Crocosmia, Aquilegia* and bluebells. Each year she uses her limited space to add a few new kinds of dried flowers to the billows indoors. This year the small space beside the greenhouse is home to *Lonas inodora, Scabious stellata*, and *Moluccella laevis*, or bells of Ireland.

Lavish use of dried flowers can be an expensive pastime. But following Lisa's example, a regular stroll round the garden with the secateurs can extend summer throughout the year.

1993

First public opening at Llidiardau

Next Sunday, 16 July, offers a rare treat for garden visitors, in the form of a brand new entrant to the National Gardens Scheme, Plas Llidiardau, seven miles south-east of Aberystwyth on the Llanilar to Trawsgoed road. Formerly the ancestral home of the Parry family, it stood neglected for many years until the 1950s, when many locals recall the massive achievements of the next owners, the Pughs, in reinstating the drive from an impenetrable overgrowth of rhododendrons. More recently it served for a while as a country restaurant, then ten years ago it came on the market yet again. The present owners, Gary Taylor and Laura Stalbow, lost no time in setting about the garden, and the fruit of their ten years' labour is now on display.

It is a novelty in itself that such a garden, expertly tended and extending to seven acres, should be the work of a couple in their thirties, more awe-inspiring still when the fact that they also have two young chidren is taken into account. If there is any explanation other than their prodigious dedication to gardening, it must lie in Laura's background (her mother, too, possesses a Gardens Scheme class of garden) and in the fact that Gary does not keep office hours. When he is not working, he really does labour in his garden, all day long, for days on end.

Their first major innovation was the stone-built formal lily pond in the level croquet lawn, a feat achieved by transplanting a forty-year-old *Magnolia stellata* which just happened to be in the way, and their most recent has been an ambitious wildlife pond, built this spring in a triangle of unused ground below the terrace. Planted exclusively with native species, it looks raw and new, but is already developing an aquatic fauna. Its excavation revealed some magnificent smoothed glacial boulders and, intriguingly, an old iron cannon-ball. The overgrown kitchen garden has been reclaimed to house Laura's plant nursery, where she propagates hardy geraniums and unusual border perennials, and a vegetable garden which is a model of labour-saving order. Deep beds framed in breeze blocks and narrow beds employing paving and black polythene mulch illustrate the advantages of readily accessible, weed-free plots.

A crowning glory for the plant lover is the newly created double herbaceous border which runs northward from the house beside the kitchen garden. It would be futile to name all the fine plants among such an array, but sometimes the simplest of plantings can be the most exciting. Laura has planted leeks behind the *Ozothamnus rosmarinifolius*. Kremlin-like onion domes hover on five-foot stems, and then burst open to display a perfect sphere of flowers of palest mauve. The right-hand and most luxuriant border was planted only in 1994, a testament to the importance of really thorough soil preparation.

Gary has divided the garden into a number of colour-coded walks, with explanatory guides which are informative, scholarly and humorous too. Town or courtyard gardeners should collect the leaflet for the orange route around the house, where there is an incomparable exhibition of low-maintenance trees, shrubs and climbers, growing out through a dense weed-free layer of river gravel. The rotating clothes line, that necessary garden eyesore, has been superseded: at Llidiardau a fine mitred post of Welsh oak topped with a ball finial rotates its burden of socks and sweatshirts in the breeze. An architect at heart, Gary is someone for whom no detail is so small as to be unworthy of attention.

Forty-five members of the Dutch Royal Horticultural Society recently included Llidiardau on their itinerary through Wales. The public open day is the first opportunity for locals to see what is set to become a garden of renown.

1995

The acquisition of Llanerchaeron by the National Trust

Why does a man noted in his lifetime for the vigour with which he repelled the public from his land, then leave that same property to the public in his will? Perhaps because in giving it to the National Trust he could be confident that it would be conserved for future generations, and that visitors, though welcome, would be kept on a tight (if invisible) rein.

The property in question is Llanaeron, or perhaps more properly, Llanerchaeron estate, two miles up-river from Aberaeron. There is an unpretentious pink stuccoed house with good proportions and broad eaves which was designed by John Nash in 1794, during his 'Cardiganshire period'. Aberaeron and Hafod also received his attention at this time.

Adjoining it, through a belt of trees, is an extensive set of estate buildings, barns, storesheds, workshops, stables, byres and kennels, the latter until recently home of the Llanaeron Otter Hounds. One of the last such packs to be disbanded as public opinion veered in favour of the otter, I am told these hounds were hunting the Ystwyth Valley at Llanfarian as recently as 1969.

There was also a lake, now silted up, with wooded surrounds, meandering walks, and a footbridge linking to an island in its middle. Conduits from the lake supplied water to the farm, the two huge walled gardens, and to a water-powered private electricity-generating system.

The estate has undergone little change other than that wrought by decay in the last hundred years or so. By-passed by modernization, it evokes echoes of a time when the estate teemed with workers under the enlightened and enormously competent leadership of Mary Ashby Mettam, who married the elderly squire John William Lewes in 1841, was widowed fourteen years later, and remained mistress of Llanerchaeron for a staggering total of seventy-six years.

On an evening excursion with the Cardiganshire Horticultural Society we inspected the walled gardens now deep in weeds except for a few areas where valiant volunteers, under the direction of Dr John Savidge, have undertaken a little conservation gardening. Remnant stock of plants once grown for the house—gladioli, lily of the valley and antirrhinums—can still be found and are being preserved; they may represent old varieties now rare in cultivation. There are old espaliered apple trees, a prey to woolly aphids and fungal die-back, a quince, some plums and pears trained against the walls, and one or two old rambling roses about the paths. Clipped box hedges, about one foot high, margin the main path, and alpine strawberries compete with wild vegetation about the small, deep, now empty dipping pond. The wooden greenhouses, hot frames and cold frames have, as these inevitably do, collapsed, but a small leap of imagination restores all to order, luxuriance and fruitfulness.

It is to be hoped that this is just what the National Trust with a mighty click of the fingers will achieve. Certainly in other National Trust properties, suth as Barrington Court in Somerset, a mouth-watering walled kitchen garden is maintained which is every bit as alluring as the Gertrude Jekyll borders.

However, before flexing their muscles, the Trust have arranged an open day at which the public will be able to take in the special character and atmosphere before renovation of the property begins. They hope that it will stimulate local interest, and are keen to see any old photographs or documents relating to the estate which may be in the possession of local people.

1991

Footnote: It proved to be five years before the National Trust obtained the finance to commence a serious programme of restoration at Llanerchaeron.

Beryl Birch thrives at altitude

Thirty years ago, when Beryl Birch and her husband bought a portable bungalow situated on a sheep-cropped hillside at 800 feet above sea level at Ponterwyd, she probably never even considered a future in which she would be opening her garden to the public. This July, however, sees her début in the National Gardens Scheme. New recruits to the scheme in our area are few and far between, so I was eager to preview the garden before her open day on Wednesday 28 July.

Number 7 Maes yr Awel started life as a Terrapin bungalow, portable housing put up to accommodate the engineers working on Nant y Moch reservoir. Some of its neighbours were indeed folded up and taken elsewhere, and as time passed the present housing estate of council homes and old people's bungalows brought services and communal clipped grass to the development.

Mrs Birch's temporary house, meanwhile, took deeper and deeper root, extending in various directions with kitchen and conservatory, and the garden began, haltingly, to take shape among the mature birch trees on the hillside. Pausing regularly at Percy Thrower's Garden Centre on trips to the Midlands, she bought ornamental conifers, roses, herbaceous plants and thus began a personal investigation of the range of plants tolerant of thin acid soil, wind and altitude.

Hybrid tea roses do not, on the whole, like this situation, but Mrs Birch grows 'Albertine' over a pergola and has found an exquisite soft pink floribunda-type rose which loves it here and wears a cascade of blossom above shiny bright green leaves from now until September.

Junipers, prostrate and erect, golden, blue and green, flourish, as do many different varieties of cupressus, yew and holly. Colour is provided by *Spiraea japonica* 'Little Princess', *Potentilla fruticosa* in many shades, and quite a variety of hardy geraniums. Summer bedding plants, in borders and containers add to the array, and you may find some recent introductions like the magically fragrant chocolate plant, *Cosmos atrosanguineus,* in an urn near the house.

The garden paths lead one to a series of enclosed spaces, with pools, fountains, small lawns and patios. Living walls of clipped trees form the boundaries. It is perhaps in the range of carefully trimmed evergreens that this garden has most to teach us. In a confined garden many of Beryl's purchases could have got thoroughly out of hand were it not for regular trimming. Structure and topiary is largely the work of her partner Nick Stead, and includes a multi-hued flat-topped hedge in variegated holly, a Christmas tree fashioned like a flat-topped circular coffee table, arches of yew, deodar and hawthorn. Anyone with a loose-textured undisciplined Leylandii hedge should pay homage here. Regular clipping has produced a wall which is dense, green and as solid to lean on as a carthorse.

1993

Judging a 'best garden' competition

There are some gardeners who can never be lured to the show bench. Their enthusiasm lies in creating harmony in colour and perhaps in specialisms not catered for by competition classes, in trees and shrubs, alpines, or delicate occupants of the greenhouse. Vegetable gardeners also have much more to display at home. There is something extremely pleasing about the orderly charm of a weed-free vegetable garden with its successional plantings of summer and winter vegetables, sequenced to feed a family for the year.

It is to give due credit to these gardening skills that some shows also run a 'best garden' competition, limited for the sake of the judges' stamina to their own local area. I learnt just how demanding such a competition can be when I was asked to judge the 'best garden' classes for the Llancynfelin Show.

Accompanied by a member of the show committee (an essential guide and navigator) I must have spent nearly six hours, much of it in sheeting rain, inspecting some thirty diverse gardens or container displays in Tre'r-ddôl, Taliesin and Eglwysfach.

Despite the considerable personal freedom accorded to judges, the range of entrants was difficult to compare, and I found the responsibility a heavy one. In judging the window boxes and hanging baskets I gave considerable weight to the way in which these displays complemented the setting in which they were found. But how to rate the relative importance of inspired artistic composition and first-rate horticultural condition?

The flower gardens, too, exhibited diverse charms. There were traditional cottage gardens with rambler roses, and borders overflowing with lysimachia, phlox, evening primroses and hardy geraniums. There were meticulously tended gardens with neat displays of annuals such as salvia, lobelia and alyssum edging the beds, perfectly weed-free lawns with modern sweeping curves and borders of choice junipers and chamaecyparis.

Once again I found it helpful to look at how the gardener had made the most of the resources of his or her plot and integrated it into the landscape. Often landscape features were downright intrusive. Many gardens in these villages boasted an unexpected outcrop, a platy sheet of rock sticking up at a crazy angle, or a steep and stony bank where the house is let into the hillside. I found imaginative use of terracing to contain alpines, cascading plants or water features. In one garden in Eglwysfach the owners had an unpromising back garden dominated by two large sloping outcrops sticking up where lawn and shrubs might normally be found. Undaunted they had excavated down the slope of the rock face to create a charming rock-bound natural pond deep enough for water lilies to thrive.

Certain local wildflowers are frequent denizens of the older gardens. Royal ferns, *Osmunda regalis*, doubtless descendants of those on nearby Cors Fochno, are found in the gardens of many older properties, and luxuriant patches of the greater celandine, *Chelidonium majus,* fill many awkward corners under trees and hedges. While nobody should augment their garden by digging up wild plants, it is pleasing to see these native species still accorded value by local gardeners. Neither can readily be bought outside of specialist plant nurseries these days.

1990

august

Pant-yr-Holiad garden

Pant-yr-Holiad garden near Rhydlewis is tucked away in a secret valley about three miles inland from Llangrannog. It looks, from above, like any other small Welsh farmstead, with a few cows in the valley bottom field, an old caravan housing a family of geese, and mixed deciduous woodland clothing the steep valley sides.

However, those who went there on a hot Sunday in late July toiled along narrow and sloping paths in that woodland to discover many changes wrought in some seventeen years of gardening by Geoffrey and Brenda Taylor.

As might be expected of a garden wrested from a bramble-smothered hillside, the longest established and lushest plants are to be found nearer to the house and to the richer, flatter and reliably moister land near the valley bottom. The ambitions of gardeners, though, are rarely satisfied while there is still space to expand, and over the years the owners have extended their domain up the hillside.

For rhododendron buffs this is a place of pilgrimage: many fine species rhododendrons lurk among the native woodland, and there are real rarities to be seen, like *Rhododendron trichocladum*, a shrub grown from wild seed, delicately decked with clusters of discreetly beautiful flowers of that browny-yellow flushed with pink more commonly associated with tropical orchids. There are new hybrids, too. Mr Taylor has added three of his own to the thousands of registered cultivars. 'Holiad Brenda', 'Brenda's Choice' and 'Holiad Michelle' immortalize the ladies of his family.

For the non-specialist visitor there are the sinuous paths through woods loud with chiff-chaff song, and the spectacle of familiar ornamental Japanese maples grown twenty years large. Climb right to the top of the garden to see the exquisite green and cream striped snake-bark branches of *Acer grosseri hersii* and the extraordinary gleaming red coiled-prawn flowers on the *Grevillea rosmarinifolia*.

Newest project is Brenda's 'Long Border', which is indeed long, and cut at a steady incline into the side of the hill. Here new plantings are only recently established in stony beds cut back into the hill such that their back margin is some four foot of vertically cut rubbly subsoil and rock. These herbaceous beds are arranged by colours and should fill out in blocks of yellow, pink, blue and white. They are as yet widely spaced and panting a little in the summer drought. On attaining the summit of the Long Border, some 700 feet above sea level, we are invited, by a bronze plaque, to rest awhile and contemplate the view and the faintly chiding couplet

'If our efforts are decried—
please remember that we tried!'

Descending the hill one passes small clearings in the native grass containing new groups of hybrid lilies and diverse ornamental shrubs, including a well-grown *Enkianthus campanulatus*. Near the old mill pool an area of herb garden runs fragrant riot, and narrow paths and grassy walks twine among well-grown species rhododendrons, acers, hydrangeas, camellias, and small herbaceous and alpine beds.

The tour ends as it began, by the farmhouse clothed in a triple tangle of climbers. Before the white-flowered *Jasminum officinale* fills the August valley with its heavy scent, the house blooms twice already, thanks to the clematis and *Vinca major* twined within its framework.

1989

Organic gardening at Cemmaes

Fifteen years ago Harry and Olivia Chandler would have been described as self-sufficiency migrants, inspired by writers such as John Seymour and perhaps *The Good Life* to eke an ecologically-sound living from the land. Many such original migrants have long since dropped back into city life; those who remain almost invariably have extended the concept to include some cash-generating activities beyond the confines of the home.

Harry and Olivia's nine-and-a-half-acre smallholding, Gwalia, is tucked away in a depression in the hills beneath the Cemmaes windfarm, on a sinuous rabbit-rich lane which threads its way from Cemmaes to Commins Coch. Here they produce all their vegetable requirements for the year, and keep goats, hens and bees. That additional cash necessary to meet the family's needs comes from a sideline in Organic Bed and Breakfast, visitors being entirely fed from the holding.

When Olivia first undertook the leap into serious vegetable growing she had little gardening experience, and adopted as her gardener's bible *Grow Your Own Vegetables* by Lawrence Hills. Following from the outset the principles outlined by this author, she soon became a member of HDRA, the Henry Doubleday Research Association, and it is in support of this organization that she now opens her garden to the public, as a part of the annual HDRA Members' Gardens Opening Scheme in August.

As Olivia explained to me, her chief purpose in showing her garden is to reassure the doubters that garden chemicals and pesticides really are not necessary. Nor is potting compost and peat. In her greenhouse the seed bed is composed of sieved organic-rich soil from last year's compost heap. Tomatoes, cucumbers, lettuce, Swiss chard and spinach grow in raised beds on the earth floor, and the occasional outbreak of greenfly is destroyed by a spray application of washing-up liquid.

Outside she follows a four-stage crop rotation between four separate plots. In the first year of the cycle, manure is rotovated into the ground and potatoes 'Wilja' and 'Desiree' planted. In the following three years hoeing alone keeps the soil clean, and peas and beans in year two are followed by brassicas (members of the cabbage family) in year three and finally root vegetable in year four. Where time and space permit she will fit in a crop of buckwheat as green manure. This is turned into the soil where it grew to enhance the nitrogen and organic content. There is also space for courgettes, onions and a luxuriant strawberry bed, and for gooseberries, currants, plums and cherries.

Visitors can wander from the garden to the quarter-acre lake, brilliant with yellow flags and blue damsel flies, great and lesser spearwort, and fine water lilies from Gregynog. But a visit would scarcely be complete without a detour to the toilet, where handpainted lizard, mole, wasp, snail, centipede and frog await the buttocks on the wooden seat.

1994

A horticultural haven at the Royal Welsh

While many people go to the Royal Welsh Show primarily for the spectacular animals and for the sense of theatre of the shearing, ballooning, motor cycling or lubricious dance displays by the Young Farmers Club, a steady stream detour to the margin of the show-grounds for the quieter joys of the Flower Tent. Here are competitive displays of flowers and vegetables, massed displays of floral art and perhaps most appealing of all, a large number of trade stands, exhibiting and also retailing plants to the public. Many displays are of quality and imagination comparable with those to be seen at Chelsea, but provide a much better opportunity for Welsh gardeners to get our chosen plants home uncrushed and without one arm stretched longer than the other.

On my leisurely circuit of the tent I was particularly entranced by the bonsai display by Pinewood Bonsai of Formby, Liverpool. A long table displayed a large number of these miniaturized trees, many appearing of great antiquity, gnarled roots reaching down around jagged rocks, leaves tiny but forming an entirely natural-looking canopy. *Acer palmatum* is clearly a very popular subject for the art of bonsai, and young seedlings were on sale for a modest sum for those brave enough to start their own bonsai programme. Another acer, *Acer buergerianum,* was perhaps more striking still, with its intricately formed dark green leaves. Most trees can be successfully treated and especially charming were a small elm, *Ulmus parvifolia,* and an extraordinarily natural-looking grove of tiny swamp cypresses, *Taxodium distichum,* in a single large bowl.

Across the way the eyes reeled at the cacophany of colour on D. D. Thomas & Son of Ammanford's massed display of camellia-flowered begonias. Reds, oranges, pinks and yellows of extraordinary vividness and vast diameter jostled with two-tone versions, their petals delicately rimmed with red.

Dibleys of Efenechtyd, Llanelidan, Ruthin, were there with their regular medal-winning display of *Streptocarpus,* African violets and related plants. Easily propagated by leaf cuttings, the varieties of colour, shade and form are legion.

Many other trade exhibitors were from over the border and some from far away. Burncoose Nurseries from Redruth in Cornwall, and Hillmans of Boundary Avenue, Rushden, Northants, offered exquisite displays of hybrid lilies and are collecting orders for dispatch when the bulbs are dormant in the autumn.

I learnt of the existence of two less remote nurseries well worth a detour on a trip to England, to add to my long-standing favourite, Rushfields of Ledbury. Llanbrook Alpine and Wildflower Nursery of Hopton Castle, Clunton, Shropshire, had an enticing display of hardy plants all grown in peat-free compost. Many unusual small plants were there and I particularly liked a diminutive lemon-yellow *Lysimachia* whose precise species neither of us could recollect. For cactus fanciers, D. & J. H. Tate of Heldon Nurseries, Ashbourne Road, Spath, Uttoxeter, offered a dazzling choice. Beside the huge display plants, Mrs Tate was doing a brisk trade in small cacti and succulents at three for £3.25. To augment deaths in my *Lithops* collection I was delighted to be able to select from at least eight different species of these unusual 'stone plants', and a dizzy range of cacti and succulents of all kinds.

1992

Something gruesome at Gregynog

I sometimes feel garden sculpture falls into two distinct categories: that which must be guarded from the attentions of unscrupulous thieves, and that which one longs for them to take away.

In the former category were the ornaments which many will have admired, over the years, at the annual Trawsgoed Garden Party, in the charming water garden which cascades down towards the formal lawn to the south of the house. Commissioned by the mother of the present Lord Lisburne in the 1930s, it originally boasted an alligator and frog, in addition to the pelican and the handsome lead crane which appears to be stepping out into the open water from the skunk cabbages in the shallows. The alligator and frog I have never seen: they were stolen many years ago. The crane was, however, an old familiar, securely fastened by a rod between its legs to a concrete base in the soil. This year it has had to be removed after attempts had been made to wrench it from the ground by thieves or vandals willing to destroy or damage the prize they sought to steal.

At Gregynog, near Newtown, the former home of the Misses Gwendoline and Margaret Davies and now a study centre belonging to the University of Wales, I found sculptures whose disappearance would cause me less disquiet. There is a group of shallow dishes beneath a fine *Chamaecyparis lawsoniana*, disposed like three bowls upon the mown grass. These are 'Elemental Vessels' by Helen Jones. Each is about three feet in diameter, rough textured and composed, apparently, of salt, coal, earth, leaves and resin. They have filled most unappealingly with rainwater and form a murky green habitat for mosquito larvae and diving water beetles. Steep-sided, they would be a drowning hazard to any bird attempting to drink from the surface.

The gardens at Gregynog are certainly worth a visit, and are open daily at no charge. The view from the terrace in front of the black-and-white false-timbered house (closer inspection reveals it to be clad in an intricate skin of black-and-white ornamented concrete.) offers a fine panorama of conifers, chiefly wellingtonia, Douglas fir and chamaecyparis. A detour down the dell brings one to fine established clumps of *Gunnera manicata,* peltiphyllums, and the variety of *Ligularia* 'Gregynog Gold' made famous by the Misses Davies. It is a shock, therefore, when returning on a gentle path through the woods, suddenly to meet a giant resin hand propped up upon its severed wrist in front of a fine *Sequoiadendron giganteum*. The hand is grey and shows severe brachydactyly or shortness of fingers. I persuaded my companion to seat herself on the ball of its gesturing thumb but this in no way improved the scene, which could not be described as harmonious, shocking or even funny.

I do not feel that garden sculpture should necessarily be purely representational or traditional. But only good form and line looks at ease among natural shapes. Severed body parts, or kitsch constructions such as wishing wells and miniature windmills, are all in danger of appearing yet more tawdry in a beautiful setting.

1995

Footnote: As a result of this article it became apparent that the murky bowls, at least, belonged to a temporary exhibition which had failed to leave at the appointed time.

CAT tackles the slug

Slug paradise is perhaps the best description of this changeable, wet summer. Undeterred by drying winds or blazing sunshine, they graze all day long, climbing to the very extremities of plants in search of flavour and variety. In these conditions they will shin to the very tops of my *Cosmos bipinnatus* and the newly opened scarlet-flowered *Lobelia cardinalis,* stripping off the stem surface as they go. It is not unusual to find one bivouacked in a gladiolus flower three feet above ground on damp rainy days.

It was with particular interest, therefore, that I collected a factsheet on the subject of slug control on a recent, rainy visit to the Centre for Alternative Technology (CAT) at Machynlleth. Gardening here is carried on according to strict organic principles, and moreover on a thin-soiled shaly site that few would select as promising gardening terrain. Adjoining the cultivated areas is a rich natural vegetation of bramble, ragwort, hogweed and coarse grasses, a seemingly endless reservoir of molluscan raiders.

It would be nice to report a slug-free garden, tribute to the efficency of environmentally friendly methods. Sadly this is too much to hope. I saw individual lettuces reduced to a bristly tuft of midribs quite stripped of leaves, and cabbages lacy from the ravages of caterpillar and slug. Other similar plants, however, remained in palatable condition, and this perhaps illustrates what can be achieved, an equilibrium in which pest numbers do leave a part of the crop for the gardener.

Regular hand picking is the basis of the CAT method, and the yield of a night's sortie with a torch is then fed to the appreciative ducks. Day traps, which enable slugs to congregate near their food source, are also effective provided their lodgers are regularly collected and removed. Between the rows of vegetables the gardener lays lengths of slabwood from the local sawmill, the round-sided bits which are the marginal pieces produced in cutting a series of planks. Laid flat-face down on the soil they create a pocket of cool and moisture and slugs will burrow beneath them for day shelter. Of course, if not regularly lifted and cleared, these 'traps' act as safe havens from which the marauders return nightly to denude their food plants.

Unique to CAT is the comfrey method of slug control. This utilizes the attraction to slugs of limp, wilting comfrey leaves in the early part of the year. The gardener piles comfrey leaves in the centre of a plot about a week before planting in spring. Within about five days great numbers of slugs have followed one another's slime trails to the comfrey and it and they can then be removed. A barrier margin of comfrey leaves around the newly planted plot will then decoy any new slugs moving in from round about. Sadly this appealing solution becomes ineffective from early July onwards. When I visited in August there was clear evidence of slugs sauntering straight past the wilted comfrey and setting about the vegetables. The CAT factsheet remarks that 'this disadvantage is a minor one because by July seedlings are big enough to withstand attack and the hot dry weather inhibits slug activity'. In the light of this wet summer they may wish to consider deleting this comforting observation.

1993

Bring on the naked ladies

There is no time to be lost in buying and planting colchicums and crocuses for autumn flowering. Within a mere four to six weeks the new dormant bulbs will thrust up their elegant stemless pastel-shaded flowers, so striking in their pristine freshness at a time when much is tired and worn in the shrub foliage and borders.

To the casual glance, crocuses and colchicums are remarkably similar, resulting, confusingly, in the common name of autumn crocus for *Colchicum autumnale*. In fact, while crocuses are flat-cormed members of the iris family, best known for their spring-flowering members meticulously arranged in municipal bedding schemes throughout the land, colchicums have elongate or oval corms and belong to the lily family. They are distinguished by a total absence of leaves at the time of flowering and are thus perhaps better remembered by their other common names, 'naked ladies' or 'naked boys'.

Each corm produces a cluster of flowers, in the case of *Colchicum byzantinum* as many as twenty pale purple star flowers, and since the corms increase freely to form groups, established colchicums can make an impressive display. They have one drawback, which certainly explains the absence of colchicum bedding schemes. After flowering they must remain in the ground to produce long, untidy ovate to strap-shaped leaves the following spring. Since these are quite large, up to ten inches long in *Colchicum autumnale*, they are much less suitable for naturalizing in lawns and may also be a hazard in borders, since the collapsing leaves may smother smaller plants before they wither and die down in late July.

Nonetheless, naked ladies, skilfully situated in a sunny gap in the shrub border are an arresting treat in the autumn garden, comparable with the delight of a well-placed clump of nerines.

Autumn leaves or a late-summer ground cover of green make an ideal foil for the delicate wineglass-shaped blooms. A specialist catalogue can offer a score of different varieties of colchicum ranging in colour from violet through rose to pure white. Only the double-bloomed varieties such as *Colchicum autumnale* 'Roseum Plenum' disappoint me for their loss of purity of form.

True crocuses which flower in autumn offer a similar range of colours (why, I wonder, are there no autumn crocuses in familiar yellow or gold?) and their narrow spiky leaves with central white stripe emerge more or less with the flower, and must remain until the following spring. *Crocus speciosus*, a light blue flower with dark veins and orange anthers, is popular for naturalizing in grass, though in a mild winter the needs of the crocus leaves can lead to an untidy, unkempt lawn. Better for nooks in a warm rockery, for they are not so hardy, are *Crocus goulimyi*, remarkably like its spring-flowering cousin *Crocus tommasinianus* or the large-flowered *Crocus sativus*, the saffron crocus, from which saffron is commercially and expensively produced by plucking the stamens.

For those who sorely regret the lack of a yellow crocus in autumn, nature can offer one substitute, *Sternbergia lutea*, actually a member of the daffodil family, but remarkably like a yellow crocus.

1992

Survival of the bitterest

In the fourteenth century, Bishop Basil asserted that roses acquired their thorns as a result of The Fall. Had he been a gardener, he might have reached another conclusion.

Thorns are one of the ways in which plants protect themselves against grazing and browsing animals, and rose varieties with few soft thorns like 'Marguerite Hilling', or none at all in the case of the exquisite pink but rather floppy 'Zéphirine Drouhin' are enthusiastically consumed by sheep, cattle or goats. These are the exceptions, selected by rose breeders for their unthreatening form, but in real need of the protection of domesticity. Wild roses are well armed for good reason.

Also palatable, but well protected, are other popular garden plants such as the berberis, whose ferocious thorns lurk inconspicuously among soft leaves, and the holly, which, interestingly, grows almost thornless leaves near the top of taller trees. I do not know if the Longleat giraffes browse upon holly, but certainly the tree is not adapted to prevent it.

Mammalian herbivores are not, of course, the only threat to plant health and many plants have achieved unpalatability to at least certain pests. Nasturtiums, for example, are a long way down a slug's list of favourite snacks, but can be devastated to a mass of umbrella-spoke ribs by the cabbage-white butterfly. Densely hairy surfaces seem to protect leaves of some plants from slugs and snails, but are no deterrent to the piercing mouth-parts of aphids.

Actually poisonous leaves are another excellent protective mechanism which has developed in many plants. Tannins in leaves are not merely distasteful but interfere with caterpillar digestive systems and stunt their growth. Very poisonous plants are the milkweed of North America which contains cardiac glycosides, toxic to the heart, and the common ragwort, *Senecio jacobaea*, which has leaves rich in toxic alkaloids. Both flourish in over-grazed pasture because stock avoid them.

Interestingly in each case, at least one kind of caterpillar has evolved a means to resist the damaging effects of the poison and incorporate it into its own tissues. The caterpillar of the monarch butterfly eats milkweed, and the handsome black and yellow banded caterpillars of the cinnabar moth consume ragwort. Both assimilate the borrowed poison and are, as a result, highly unpalatable to birds.

september

Probus—an example to us all

The only drawback to going on holiday is the unavoidable aura of mild neglect which greets one on one's return. Choice plants have blown over, or bloomed unappreciated, the lawn needs cutting and the patio tubs are dry. Almost before the suitcases are unpacked a rescue mission is called for. Some gardeners take only winter holidays to avoid this problem. However, in doing so, they miss the opportunity to glean inspiration from the work of others.

On my holiday in Cornwall I visited the Demonstration Garden at Probus near St Austell, seven and a half acres of permanent exhibits illustrating garden techniques and ideas. This garden was established in 1970, by the extraordinarily astute Cornwall County Council, on an open-field site on the flank of a sunny hill just outside the village. For an annual fee of £3 the local gardeners may visit as frequently as they wish, while clarifying their own garden designs. Classes are run by the Centre for Rural Studies and there are horticultural advisers regularly on call. I paid £1 for my entry, and wandered rapt, notebook in hand, desperate to recall as much as possible from a single visit.

In the upper garden were demonstrations of cultivation techniques. Separate vegetable plots each grew rows of onions, carrots, beetroot and lettuce, cultivated according to different regimes of fertilizer, manure and compost over the past nineteen years. Prize-worthy vegetables on the manure and compost plots compared with poor runts on the light Cornish soil. I was interested to note only marginal improvement given by compost plus Growmore, in comparison with compost alone. I emerged even more devoted to compost, especially where beetroot and lettuce are concerned.

Nearby were five shrub gardens mulched with grass cuttings, gravel or forest bark, treated with simazine, or hand weeded. Identical shrubs in each plot demonstrated the importance of a thick insulating mulch in reducing winter losses to frost, and showed how damaging hand weeding can be to shallow-rooted plants. In some cases size increase had been three-fold where roots were left undisturbed.

In the lower garden landscaped beds exhibit many categories of plant, for rock and scree gardens, herbaceous borders, windy hills or shady places, and collections of bamboos, eucalyptus, hydrangeas, hebes and heathers. There is no aspect of gardening neglected at Probus, with clear demonstrations on how to plant a tree, prune your shrubs or build a pond and pave a path.

The Cornish are indeed lucky to have such a source of inspiration on their doorstep and, of course, they pay for it through county funds. But when one considers how important gardens are to the amenity of any town or village, and how much the collection is used for reference by architects, planners and garden designers, it is surely public money very well spent.

1989

Cultivated ruins at Manorbier Castle

It may be considered sacrilege to say so, but I sometimes get rather bored with the extensive acres of well tended and neatly edged grass which traditionally surround British historic ruins. Abbeys and castles have a uniform tidiness about them, no bramble-choked descending stepways to tease the imagination, few owl-infested ivy-clad towers. Though much has been lost during centuries of decay, that which remains seems stripped of its mystery, polished clean, safely repointed and impeccably lawned.

This summer I visited Valle Crucis Abbey near Llangollen, a sister Cistercian institution to our own well-kept Strata Florida Abbey, and strolled, guidebook in hand, around the site. From this book I learnt that someone had built a rather cosy-looking eighteenth-century farmhouse nestling up within the ancient walls. In 1879, with high-principled zeal, it was demolished to make way for more grass.

At Manorbier, west of Tenby, is a far friendlier castle where the old stone seems less brutally exposed, more loved. Gaunt from without, its thirteenth-century curtain wall is laced with ivy which seems to rush up from the woods beneath. However, the visitor who crosses the moat and passes through the Norman gatehouse pauses in astonishment. To the left, snuggled up beneath the wall, is a comfortable cottage, with fuchsias and roses round the door. All round the margin of the inner ward, cosseted and sheltered by that most excellent wall, is a fine herbaceous border.

Manorbier was acquired in the 1880s by J. R. Cobb, who had himself been brought up in the fortified manor house of Broughton Castle, near Banbury in Oxfordshire. Recognizing the potential of a good wall, he built the cottage, renovated much of the gatehouse and towers, and began the garden we see today. It is not an exotic border, but is composed of a constellation of long-established garden favourites, shrubs, robust perennials and an infilling of tender bedding towards the front. A large Russian vine, *Polygonum baldschuanicum,* climbs up one inner wall, while sumach, tree mallow, buddleia, rambler and rugosa and tea roses jostle in the back of the border. Wild valerian and hemp agrimony grow in crevices on the old wall and have been allowed to take their place in the border alongside rose of Sharon, hydrangeas, fuchsias, ice-plant, artemisia, lavender, santolina and catmint. Dogwood and golden variegated *Euonymus japonicus* brighten awkward corners of the old ruins, while godetias, mixed nicotiana, candytuft, nasturtiums, *Begonia semperflorens* and pink lavatera and dahlias are interplanted with the perennials.

None of this gardening can have seriously impaired Manorbier's impact as a castle, for it was selected by the BBC to represent both Cair Paravel and the witch's castle in the dramatization of *The Lion, the Witch and the Wardrobe*. Only archaeologists, eager to excavate unchecked, may find themselves in conflict with this type of use.

1993

Preserving plant cultivars and memories

My recent articles musing about my climbing rose, perhaps 'American Pillar' or 'Maria Liesa', brought forth an unprecedented correspondence, stirring recollection among many readers.

These letters illustrate an importance of flowers quite separate from their botanical uniqueness. They are the pegs on which we hang memories, associations of friends and relatives, events of years gone by.

One reader, Mr Sherrington of Ystrad Meurig, recollected the 'American Pillar' rose as vastly popular in the 1920s and 1930s in suburban London. He attributed its disappearance to the devastation of the blitz. Finding that pre-war climber again, flourishing eighteen years ago in West Dorset, it is little wonder he propagated it from cuttings and brought it to Ystrad Meurig.

Other readers give pedigrees interlinked with their families to their favourite roses. J. J. Richards, also of Ystrad Meurig, described a rose history stretching back to his wife's grandmother's sixty years of gardening. This correspondent also describes the gardener's bereavement, the loss of a plant cherished for its own sake and for its associations, donated by a friend now dead, and consequently almost irreplaceable. In this case the rose was 'Ami Quinard' a bush rose with dark red double flowers and serrated leaves, which bloomed for weeks in summer. He also seeks, on behalf of a friend, two long lost roses from America, the Crucifixion Rose (white with a red cross on every flower), and the American Admiral (a double deep red whose flowers turned almost black after a week). Each quest, despite appeals to nurseries and the American Rose Society, has been unsuccessful.

This tale illustrates the role of the recently formed NCCPG, the National Council for the Conservation of Plants and Gardens, a sadly clumsy acronym. Less than one third of named varieties of garden plants appear on any nursery's list, and while the rest may survive somewhere in cottage gardens or great collections, for the most part they survive incognito.

As those who know their names and history die or move house, the chances of these plants being rediscovered fades fast. Recent correspondence in *The Garden* showed how the name 'Miss Wilmott' has been incorrectly applied to many shades of *Potentilla nepalensis* and the true cherry-pink cultivar was all but lost. Of course, individual readers then cropped up, in proud possession of the real 'Miss Wilmott', and a proper collection of potentillas is now being formed.

The NCCPG is the instigator of this system by which these 'National Collections' of all cultivated members of one or several genera are being grown and curated in private and public gardens throughout Britain. On visiting my old college, Wolfson College in Oxford, I found it now designated holder of the National Collections of *Lysimachia* and *Ceratostigma*. Almost as gratifying as this serious contribution to plant conservation was the discovery that even college fellows supremely ignorant of gardening matters took enormous pride in this collegiate claim to fame.

1991

Gardening on sand at Ynyslas

There are few gardens more wind- and salt-buffeted than the garden of Moel Ynys at Ynyslas. The old house stands just behind the sand-dunes, sheltered to an extent by one of those odd jagged outcrops of Aberystwyth grits which poke up here and there through the flat land around the Dyfi Estuary. Its history goes back several hundred years, as a farm, a coaching inn on the route to Aberdyfi, and as an officer's mess during the last war. For the last forty years it has been the home of Mrs Dorothy Toler who, with her husband, created a garden where rough sandy ground and makeshift army buildings stood before.

It is not an exotic garden, but a calm and orderly one which feels as if it has always been there in defiance of its surroundings. The plants and shrubs which grow here get no special cosseting, but are chosen for their hardiness in this situation. Their diversity should give hope to the gardener starting out in a similar setting, but as Mrs Toler pointed out to me, patience is needed, for plants in her garden grow so much more slowly on the thin dry skin of sandy soil, even if they are not actually scorched and cut back by wind and salt.

The key to the charm of this garden is the use of quite ordinary plants which show no trace of windburn or distress. The garden is contained within a hedge of mature *Euonymus japonicus* whose glossy green lustrous leaves contrast with the bleached greens of marram grass and reeds nearby. The front of the house is encased in ivy and Virginia creeper, *Parthenocissus tricuspidata,* which have to be trimmed back regularly lest they block the windows. The rocky outcrop behind the house is also enrobed in vigorous ivy; left untrimmed it is now a mass of flowers and a magnet for bees. Later it will be green and black with massed berries.

Around the house and flanking the front lawn are shrubs happy in this situation. *Escallonia macrantha,* the large evergreen escallonia, forms a generous mound rather than the spiky outline of many of the hybrids. Contrasting foliage is supplied by olearia, laurustinus, bay several different junipers, rosemary, hebe and cotoneaster. Shrubs in flower even in late September were *Berberis darwinii, Rosa rugosa* and honeysuckle.

Some border plants also find a place in this garden, cottage-garden favourites like marguerites, *Sedum spectabile, Lychnis coronaria,* aquilegia, wallflower, stocks and mallow. Greyish-white foliage interest is supplied by sea ragwort, or cineraria, and *Senecio greyi,* and golden flowers by *Potentilla fruticosa* and *Hypericum calycinum.* Paths are bordered by low-growing *Cotoneaster adpressa* and periwinkle, *Vinca minor.*

Despite all this variety, it came as a shock to turn a sheltered corner and find a magnificent clump of *Nerine bowdenii,* intricate pink blooms glowing in the sunshine. The context in which a plant occurs is very important to its impact. I have seen nerines growing in many suburban gardens. Here one steps back and looks at it anew.

1989

Eustoma—a new plant to gardeners

It often happens that a new season brings a hitherto unknown plant to prominence, and for me this year's new plant has been *Eustoma grandiflorum.*

I totally overlooked it in the Dobies seed catalogue, probably because it is marketed as a greenhouse annual, and as yet a conservatory is merely a twinkle in this gardener's eye. The brochure waxes lyrical: eustoma opens as a rose, expands as does a tulip, and finally resembles a poppy. So its full impact escaped me until the Royal Welsh Show where G. and H. Taylor of Audley, Stoke-on-Trent, had devoted almost their entire stand to this intriguing plant. Compact little bushes about twelve inches tall were composed of many stems each clasped by pairs of rather large, dull grey-green leaves, and topped with deep cups of pink, blue, white or purple satiny flowers. Huge lumpy golden anthers lurk, glowing, in the bottom of the cup. Unopened buds, which are numerous, are twisted around like a furled umbrella, and expand and develop colour while holding this form. Although the seed merchants describe it as an annual, here it was sold as a rhizomatous perennial: protected in a warm conservatory, the plants will go on for years.

Of course a new plant to me is likely to be commonplace elsewhere, and I soon learnt that under its old name *Lisianthus russellianum* the prairie gentian has been blooming in the wild from Colorado to Texas, tall, floppy and rather inclined to fall over. Plant breeders have been working on the new improved and compact varieties, called things like Yodel Blue, Yodel Pink and Yodel White, and creating F_1 hybrid seed.

I cannot decide whether I really like *Eustoma grandiflorum*. I am impressed but not enraptured. There is something funereal about the large, sombre leaves which is not entirely dispelled by the perfect blooms. Perhaps its best role is in flower arrangements where its leaves could be stripped away and the bloom alone contribute to the artifice of the whole. The catalogues claim that the flowers can be kept in water for a whole month. One wonders whether they would then need dusting, like plastic wreaths!

I next encountered the plant in London, as a cut flower under the florists' name of lisianthus, tall-stemmed versions this time, replete with blooms and buds. I left them as a gift upon my hostess's kitchen table. I only hope she likes them more than I do, for they are destined to be with her for some weeks yet.

1994

Tim Lewis prepares for a show

Serious horticulture show competitors are very well organized types, men usually, who will arrive on the morning of the show and extract from their car, with the apparent ease of a magician, immaculate exhibits in twenty or more classes of fruit, vegetables and flowers. Perfectly matched sets, three onions, four potatoes, trios of unbelievably long parsnips and carrots, pairs of fat little marrows as symmetrical as barrage balloons, awesomely large chrysanthemums and dahlias. It may look easy, but it is difficult to overrate the work and the meticulous forward planning which has brought about this synchronized display of excellence.

Tim Lewis, of Freshwinds, Llannon, is one such exponent of the magician's art, who makes a regular appearance at my local show, the Llanfarian and District. It was of particular interest to go behind the scenes and visit his garden six days before the competition.

We started at his home in the trim little back garden behind the house. Salt-laden wind can whistle in from the sea here, and the thick hedge is augmented by an impervious barrier of polythene-clad boarding. Lines of green windbreak fabric between rows further reduce turbulence among the foliage. Not an inch is wasted, with neat rows of strawberries, beetroots, parsnips, gooseberry bushes, scarlet runners and sweet peas. The competition parsley plants stood in pots in a big half-lidded cloche, protected from rain which might otherwise damage the heavily curly foliage.

In the house stood the vast and shapely onions, each drying on a little pedestal of cardboard. Their route to stardom began in the spring; equally critical is the fortnight's maturing, when one or more outer skin has been stripped and the onion must dry and harden in dry shade to its firm pale golden form. They must be perfectly matched in size, and without blemish. Tiny spots of softness or marbling on the surface can destroy an onion's chances of the cup. On the eve of the show, Tim will bend over each papery dry neck and bind it with raffia. Shallots sat in egg boxes in another room; their preparation requires six weeks' maturation out of the ground before the show.

For me the real eye-opener was Tim's second garden, a large level plot in the middle of the village which he cleared and began gardening five years ago. On narrow concrete paths we walked through a kaleidoscope of differently coloured dahlias and spray chrysanthemums. Here showmanship gives some ground to the uncomplicated love of flowers for their own sake. Those most intent on winning grow many plants of a limited number of varieties, thus maximizing their chances of having a perfect set of three on the appointed day. All dahlia growers seem to grow those rather dreary little dark purple pompon varieties which always win the prizes. Tim's apple-pink pompons were a delight, his white decorative dahlias 'Miss Swiss' and 'White Linda' far more pleasing to my eye than giant yellow fluorescent blooms like roadmen's overcoats.

Nearby was the deep bed containing the competition parsnips. Soon comes the suspense and excitement of gently pulling these monsters in quest of a flawless trio. The stump-rooted carrots hint only by their lightly buried tops at their eventual length and girth. The price of success will be many not-quite-matched vegetables which by-pass their chance of fame and go directly into the freezer.

1994

Sexy, slimy slug seeks similar

When I step out into the garden at night it is invariably accompanied by the crunching of snails underfoot. Principal victims are the common garden snails, *Helix aspersa,* which cluster by day in crevices in the dry stone walls or in rows in the gap between drainpipe and house. With wet and darkness they spread out to wreak havoc on the hostas, and to strip bare the stem surfaces of the *Lobelia cardinalis.*

They have a remarkable capacity to repair their shells—inspect a nest of these large brown spirally banded shells and you will often find distorted, cracked and re-cemented shells. Many are probably victims I have hurled from the garden to land violently on the road beyond. I strongly suspect they pick themselves up and hobble home.

Slugs are as numerous, most conspicuously the big gleaming black slugs often ornamented with an orange striped foot-fringe, which are properly known as *Arion ater ater.* There is a handsome brick-orange subspecies known as *Arion ater rufus* which is generally less abundant. These slugs nestle among the border plants, spreading out on enthusiastic feeding forays after heavy rain.

Less handsome and even more destructive of blooms and fruit is the netted slug, *Agriolimax reticulatus*, a small sticky, slimy, whitish-cream or brownish-yellow slug netted or mottled with dark brown and slightly keeled along the back.

Beneath the surface of the earth roots and tubers are also under attack by two species of slugs particularly devoted to the subterranean way of life. Sowerby's keeled slug, *Milax sowerbyi,* is particularly partial to potatoes, and excavates neat cavities in the tubers. The longer the potatoes remain in the ground, the more severe the damage. The garden slug, *Arion hortensis,* also burrows and will take off herbaceous plants at root level.

It is of limited comfort that there are many other species of slugs which do not harm green plants, being specialist feeders on fungi, detritus or rotten wood. One rare species, Caruana's slug, *Agriolimax caruanae,* is even a slug-eater, fast, aggressive and cannibalistic. I only wish I had some in my garden. The biggest of the keel-backed slugs, the great grey slug, *Limax maximus,* is quite harmless to garden plants, which is a relief considering its eight-inch length.

In between undertaking doomed schemes of molluscicide with metaldehyde, aluminium sulphate or beer, it is perhaps worth pausing to admire the remarkable feats of breeding in these too-successful animals. All our slugs and snails are hermaphrodite, having both male and female sex organs, so when setting out in search of a mate, any similar slug will do.

Most slugs circle around, one behind the other, gobbling each other's mucus trails before mating. Sexual athletes like the great grey slug actually mate when suspended by a thread of mucus from the branch of a tree. More bizarre still are common garden snails, which embrace slimily and then each fire into the body of the other a calcareous 'love-dart' secreted by a special dart sac in the snail's body.

Each snail, thus whipped to passion, impregnates the other, and they go their separate ways to lay and bury their cache of eggs. I once kept snails in a terrarium and made a collection of these finely sculptured darts, each a hefty quarter-inch in length. Seeing is truly believing.

1992

The delights of the dahlia

The ancient Aztec people of what is now Mexico are generally remembered as an extremely bloodthirsty civilization, given to organizing battles within their empire, not for the purpose of conquest, but in order to capture supplies of healthy adults for human sacrifice. However, they also deserve a place in horticultural history as early practitioners of intensive gardening methods, and for the domestication of the dahlia—or Cocoxochitl, as it is perhaps more properly called.

exhibitors, are, in contradiction of their name, totally without scent—huge frilled flowers, four or five to the stem, a feast for eye alone. My selection this year was an older variety, 'Old Spice', and these are puny by comparison, typically two flowers per stem, smaller, less frilly, though with a good range of colours. But here at last is the remembered scent of my grandmother's house, a heady sweet-pea pungency which wafts from a single bouquet, throughout the house.

1991

october

The show is an endangered species

It is a relief to put away, for a few months at least, the impedimenta of organizing our local show—the badges, prize cards, cups, stewards' books, rosettes and record books which keep the Llanfarian Show running from year to year.

If there is an exercise in orchestrating, for a few hours, the improbable this must surely be it, as the separate endeavours of several hundred people come together to create a huge display of excellence, exhibited to public view for just three hours on a Saturday afternoon, and then demolished and dispersed at lightning speed before dusk. Within twenty-four hours every trace is gone, exhibitors and exhibits, tables, marquee, waste paper, fences and noticeboards, and grazing cattle reclaim the peaceful meadow where it all took place.

The ephemeral nature of a village show may make it seem a small event both in space and time, but for those involved it is the culmination of months and months of endeavour. Competitors do not rest upon their laurels: on Boxing Day the masters of the giant onions-from-seed will be planting their 'Ailsa Craigs'; and exhibition leeks, probably 'Prizetaker', must be planted under glass in January. Dahlia and begonia enthusiasts will soon be lovingly preparing their tubers to last the winter in frost free sheds, and next year's giant root vetetables need expert preparation of their deep, richly manured, stone-free beds.

Among the handicraft ladies, next year's schedule of classes has already been announced, allowing for long winter evenings of crochet, tapestry and embroidery.

For the Show Secretary, too, the respite is all too brief, for in the New Year fifteen or more specialist judges must be sought out, cajoled and persuaded into committing themselves to appear the following September so that their identities may be published in the Schedule. Here is a minefield, for competitors can prove unexpectedly touchy, and every Secretary's nightmare is when competitors in a section simply melt away, unwilling to compete under the chosen judge. Expert judges from far away are safest in their anonymity, but with little reward but the lunch and the glory it is unreasonable to expect them to travel too far.

As the show draws nearer, every committee member is used to the point of destruction, collecting money to finance the show, selling raffle tickets, lending or giving a remarkable range of goods and services. To place a caterer's value on the judges' and stewards' lunch served with such panache in the Village School would seriously undermine the show funds. To rent commercially the sixty-odd trestle tables necessary to display the exhibits would far exceed the modest cost of borrowing from our own and other village halls. But this only works because the manpower to load and unload tables, the lorry and van to transport them and so many other ancillary services are provided for goodwill alone.

Every Show Day provides its crises and memorable stories. There was the year of the missing rhubarb, the occasion of the defaulting judge, the day of relentless rain when the field became a sea of mud. Perhaps most alarming of all is the spectre of getting the arithmetic wrong and giving the wrong competitor the cup. I seem to spend half the afternoon checking the sums.

Is it worth it? As long as there are able competitors, the answer must be yes. Rather more than the Welsh language, the Village Show is an 'endangered species', threatened by individual apathy and EC bureaucracy; in some parts of Wales it is already extinct. A flourishing show should be a matter of great pride.

1992

Cyclamen carpets a secluded garden

On visiting a woodland garden brilliant with azaleas and rhododendrons the visitor often wonders what will provide interest and colour when their season is past. Recently I sought the answer in Nancy Kirk's deeply secluded woodland garden, hidden in the forested Ystwyth valley between Llanafan and Pontrhydygroes.

In spring and early summer it is an experience in scent and colour, several acres of steep hillside and two narrow valley-bottom fields now forming a rambling garden of exotic trees and shrubs. Rhododendrons and azaleas, most of them grown from seed, dominate the colour schemes, and huge clumps of *Virburnum plicatum tomentosum* and thirty-foot Sargent cherry trees (also grown from seed) give contrasting form and texture. Tall sentinel eucalyptus trees hold back the ordinary forest outside the garden and huge specimen conifers, noble fir, western hemlock, Atlantic cedar and Bhutan pine rear up among the shrubs.

On a brilliant morning with the dew still heavy on the grass, my attention was immediately drawn to the big trees of *Prunus sargentii*, their drooping serrated leaves coloured as fine as any dogwood in salmon-orange and dark brilliant crimson. Nearer the house I found the smoky purple of *Cotinus coggygria* beaded with globes of silver dew long after other trees had shed theirs, the newly red, ovoid-shaped leaves held erect at the tip of each shoot and glowing vermilion in the sunlight. A huge dragonfly danced and hovered around the glade, a lone bat hawked in broad daylight, and the only sounds were the fizzing cries of the blue tits in the woodland, the mew of buzzards and the distant whisper of the river.

In such a setting one may not immediately study the deep pools of shade beneath the trees, but here was one of the autumn's greater glories, drifts of *Cyclamen neapolitanum*, naturalized over many years to form scattered dense clumps of clear mauvy pink and pure white. It is unnecessary to describe the shuttlecock shape of a cyclamen bloom, but unlike the familiar pot-plants these blooms are only about three quarters of an inch in length. Elegantly furled pointed buds are succeeded by full flowers, nodding on four-inch stems. When the flower is spent it is sloughed off and the stem coils back along its own length to make a copper-coloured five-coiled spring adpressed to the earth. Each spring clasps at its centre the ovary containing the developing seed. It is by the germination of these seeds, snowed under by the autumn fall of leaves, that the clumps increase.

Towards the end of the flowering season the leaves of the cyclamen appear, cloaking the coiled springs from view. Their ivy-like shape has promoted the new botanical name of this species, *Cyclamen hederifolium*, but growing as they do here among ground-covering ivy one is entranced by the cyclamen leaves, handsomely marbled in three shades of green like the endpapers of an old folio.

Nothing which grows in Nancy Kirk's garden receives undue cosseting, soil enrichment or application of fertilizer or manure. There are no bedding plants and little need for weeding. The secret lies in selecting species happy with the environment as it is, and adapted for their particular place in it.

1990

A giant spider's web

I often drive along Llanbadarn Road, Aberystwyth, past the freshly capped and repointed crenellated brick wall which borders the road and encloses the rear gardens of the houses of Llanbadarn village. Old pears and apples, rowan, honeysuckle and teazel peep over the top, and here and there bright yellow nasturtiums cascade towards the verge outside. The substantial bulk of Llanbadarn church breaks the skyline beyond, set about in its graveyard by tall fastigiate yews.

It is here that passing bus passengers, or the vigilant motorist, gets a fleeting surprise. Wasn't that a spider's web? And wasn't it *rather large?*

This week I circled through Llanbadarn village, stopped and looked again. Realistically suspended between the gnarled branches of an old apple tree is a five-foot web. Stand on tiptoe, and a large black spider, a handspan wide, is revealed lurking at its margin.

Here began some confusing research. My first stop was the shop, source surely of all local knowhow. But I was disappointed: a neighbour with a giant spider's web at the bottom of the garden struck no chord here.

Back to Llanbadarn Road I went. Tiptoeing for a better view, I sketched the rears of the houses beyond the gardens. It served to emphasize my difficulty, for the rear elevations of a Welsh terrace seldom bear any resemblance to the house fronts. As I concentrated on outline and chimneys, I zeroed in upon the spider-garden, closer and closer to my original target, the shop.

To its right, I hesitated. Could the house name Archnoa be some kind of pun? The sort of name an Arachnid-lover would chose? But no, placing greater trust in my own sketch-work, I banged determinedly on the door of the shop's other neighbour, Tanfynwent House. Here at last persistence was rewarded: Richard Tucker, roused from rest, acknowledged ownership with a smile.

Visiting their garden I found that the spider's web is just one of a series of increasingly ambitious garden decorations which Richard has constructed to complement his wife Molly's flowers and ornaments. Passing down the long, narrow garden I first found a wheelbarrow brimming with colourful bedding centred upon a castor oil plant 'Impala'. Beyond was a rustic pergola, built only recently with forestry poles: it looked so much more natural than the familiar machined kits. Next came an arboured seat, neatly constructed out of someone else's garden waste—boughs of Leylandii, found dumped by the river. An old mangle, its handsome cast-iron frame embossed 'W. H. Jones of Aberystwyth', has been rescued from the back of the house, freshly painted in black gloss, and now stands in the lawn, bordered by flowers and skirted by three ornamental hedgehogs.

At the bottom of the garden we came to the web, cleverly sited to focus the vista from the sunroom at the rear of the house. It was built of fresh-cut branches, twelve radial spokes, with thinner twigs lacing across the segments. The spider is a rubber one from a local toyshop. Even the apple tree proved a rare find, a 'Melrose White', the old-fashioned cooker I extolled in a recent column.

What next? Richard has recently completed a wishing well of timber, plastic and slates reclaimed from the former pigsty. Next year Molly will have garlanded it with flowers, and they rather expect to add a lifesize wooden bicycle to their collection.

1992

A flower arranger's garden

What are the qualities of a serious competitive flower arranger, the sort of person who arrives at a show with a car full of flowers, foliage, cones, fruit, shells, driftwood and reams of fabric and in the course of an hour or two assembles half a dozen prize-winning exhibits of precise size and proportion and interpretive of arcane titles such as 'Gone Fishing' or 'The Pithead Baths a Supermarket Now'? Where does this abundance of perfectly pristine plant material come from? Do flower arrangers spend a fortune at the florists?

Mary Ellis of Lerry View, Talybont, is a familiar figure at the local round of shows and a regular competitor at the Royal Welsh. Twenty years of competition have filled her two corner cupboards with cups and trophies. This autumn in the wake of her cup-winning performances I sought her out in her natural habitat.

Lerry View is a solidly built house of dressed stone which stands in its own sloping garden to one side of Talybont village. A monkey puzzle tree stands sentinel at the gateway and one approaches the house along a terraced border planted with pieris, skimmia, hydrangea and fronted with scarlet pelargoniums and the pink platy heads of ice-plants, *Sedum spectabile*. Ice-plants make frequent appearances in Mary's arrangements. Never wasteful, she later pops the flower heads back into the soil, where they root to form more plants.

It soon became apparent that essential resources for flower arranging include co-operative driver and handyman husband Herbert, and an extraordinary number of sheds and outhouses. Lerry View has at least six outhouses and two greenhouses. The old lean-to greenhouse on the end of the house contains cacti, succulents, scented-leaved pelargoniums and prize-winning tomatoes. The other, an elegant reclaimed structure formed like an upturned boat, contains a vine, a peach and more tomatoes. In the sheds, along with the trays of apples and onions and shallots, are precisely sized wooden bases and frames for flower arranging, plus boxes devoted to jars, pots, containers, vases, cones, seashells, gnarled roots, boughs and driftwood and the dried seed heads of big alliums.

The garden is a real cottage garden, tidy at the front, a working garden at the back, rather than the immaculate ideal of the magazines. Apples and vegetables have their allotted space but all the flowers have been chosen for their ornamental value to the flower arranger. Mary grows *Crocosmia masonorum* for its immaculately pleated deep green leaves, hostas, aspidistra, globe artichokes, *Euphorbia robbiae* and lady's mantle for their quality foliage. Annuals in the rear garden patch included *Cosmos* 'Seashells' with incurved tubular petals, gay yellow *Coreopsis* 'Early Sunrise', blue cornflower, honesty, love-lies-bleeding, and ornamental gourds. Essential perennials for the flower arranger include tansy for its tiny yellow button flowers, anaphalis, rue and eryngium for their flowers and leaves.

Roses are grown for their specimen blooms, and Mary also grows a few small decorative dahlias for arranging. The eucalyptus has been cut down to ensure a continued supply of attractive young blue-grey shoots. With the exception of a few sprays of florists' gypsophila and chrysanthemums, Mary Ellis's plant material comes from home.

1993

Dinefwr—has art done no harm?

It is a responsibility of putting pen to paper that the author cannot readily guess which, if any, of his pronouncements will take on a life of its own and pass down the centuries, the definitive remark. A witty epigram or vicious *double entendre* may lead to immortality; others may be factual or just tactful.

In the case of Dinefwr Park, recently acquired by the National Trust and as yet unrestored, the definitive remark goes to Capability Brown, who was consulted by the then Lord Dynevor in 1775 as to his proposals for embellishing the grounds of what was known as Newton House. With what mixture of tact and truth one cannot guess, he wrote to Lord Dynevor, 'Nature has been truly bountiful, and art has done no harm'. What he was describing was the extensive parkland above the Towy valley at Llandeilo, hilly with mature native trees, woodland and grassland, and the ancient ruin of the original medieval Dinefwr Castle perched atop the steep descent to the meandering Towy river.

In view of the fact that one round tower of that castle had, in 1660, been embellished with a circular slate-roofed summerhouse or gazebo, whose large rectangular windows in no way complemented the defensive slits in the castle it stood upon, the remark appears a diplomatic one. The sort of thing one might say to avoid criticizing an Amdega conservatory. Art may have done no harm, but it may simply not have been represented.

In any case, the summerhouse remains, Lord Dynevor retained Brown's services, and, presumably, the letter, and Brown contributed plans for a kitchen garden, garden walls, and added at least one large clump of beech trees to the landscape.

The Dinefwr estate was sold in the 1970s and has for the most part remained empty and neglected in the succeeding years. When I strolled around it last week I learnt that some of the woodland now belongs to the West Wales Naturalists Trust, while the medieval castle itself is partially scaffolded and being made safe by CADW workmen. There are some lyrical views through the parkland, where deer still roam, and some vast sweet chestnuts freely dropping their hedgehoggy fruit.

The present Plas Dinefwr is a monument to the ravages of art, and replaces the seventeenth-century Newton House which Brown would have visited. It is a dingy structure incorporating at random a variety of castle-ish features. Each corner of the rectangular house is embellished with a square-cut castellated tower set obliquely across the house's natural corners. There are some buttresses, some ornamental turrets, a three-arched structure supporting a solar on the first floor, and two tiny, rather pointless first-floor balconies. To the west of the house is a formal lawn, set with fastigiate yews—dark marginal ones framing the transverse path, four broader golden ones set around a circular fountain standing in a rectangular trough. It forms a deeply unimaginative foreground to rolling landscape framing an exquisite sunset between the hills.

It was interesting to see what garden plants survive such prolonged neglect. Against the house wall I found an old magnolia, a fine orange-berried pyracantha and a large scrambling clematis. *Polygonum baldschuanicum,* the Russian vine, slogs it out with fireweed and briars, and *Crocosmia masonorum* contends well with grass. A less happy introduction has been that of weeping beech trees: two frame the gateway to the park, and one stands by the house. Lacking the shelter of other trees these have all become gracelessly lopsided.

1992

Footnote: The National Trust has since replaced pointed turrets on the castellated corners of the Plas, and reintroduced White Park cattle to the demesne. Grounds and parts of the house are open to the public.

Grape hopes at the vineyard

On an autumn morning of billowing mist I visited a neatly tended vineyard, not on some balmy European hillside, but at Aberaeron, near the sea, where, on a north-east-facing hillside behind a modern bungalow on the Lampeter Road, Martin Lewis cultivates an acre of vines.

The grapes hang in heavy bunches, gaining in sweetness as the days pass. Using a portable refractometer, Martin regularly assays the sugar content of the fruit. He anticipates they should have reached sufficient

november

Waiting for the first frost

The frost-free October has produced some delightful combinations of late flowering and autumn colour. My dahlias still flower freely, their colours somehow even more glowing in the waning evening light than they seemed in their August perfection. Several hardy geraniums are still in bloom, and the Kaffir lilies, *Schizostylis coccinea,* glow in pink and red. There is also strident autumn colour, the hosta leaves a glowing orange-yellow, *Acer palmatum dissectum* an amazingly penetrating scarlet red. One of the finest combinations I have seen this year was the juxtaposition of *Dahlia* 'Bishop of Llandaff' and the glowing reds of a fully turned Virginia creeper. This remarkable Welsh dahlia produces numerous single ruby-red gold-centred flowers set upon wonderful bronze-red foliage. In the same idiom, the tender *Fuchsia* 'Thalia' still blooms in pots by the front door, salmon-red tubular flowers nodding above handsome bronze-green leaves.

This charmed scene cannot be expected to persist much longer: a single frost will wither all the luxuriant dahlias to black rags, and the winds will soon disperse the autumn leaves. Time to reflect that, although in many publications those little climate maps of Britain designate the entire coastal margin of Wales, along with Devon and Cornwall, as extremely mild, there is an extensive list of frost-hardy plants which I have killed through winter neglect.

The reasons for my failures lie variously with excessive wet, with the ravages of winter slugs and with dehydration during the cold snaps of the winter. Certainly there is more autumn housekeeping that I could do to improve my record.

The value of winter mulching cannot be over-estimated, for it provides a degree of insulation from cold and protection from heavy rain. Many plants are killed by cold waterlogged conditions but will tolerate a good freeze if the soil remains porous and does not become a block of ice about their roots. Consider the stress to a plant frozen in the ground yet still losing water from its evergreen foliage, and quite unable to replenish that loss. An insulating layer of bark or bracken will probably be sufficient to prevent the entire depth of the roots being frozen, while shelter will reduce the drying effects of the wind on those rare cold, dry, high-pressure days. Although it may look a little eccentric, this is why keen gardeners may actually wrap evergreen shrubs in horticultural fleece or wind-break netting for the winter.

Plants which die down entirely in the winter are too easily forgotten, but beneath ground they remain at risk from freezing and waterlogging. Although hitherto I have religiously lifted, dried and stored my dahlia tubers, I know of other gardeners who successfully leave them in the ground, covering the soil where they grow with a deep layer of autumn leaves, or even with strips of corrugated iron. A plant which I have repeatedly killed in my garden is the little pink and white daisy *Erigeron karvinskianus*. I now grow it in an outdoor pot, mulched on the surface with a thick layer of 'Lica', light pellets of volcanic ash used in insulating cements for chimney lining. The compost in the pot remains much drier than the soil, and the inert layer traps heat from the sun and slows night-time heat loss. In spring the delicate shoots have no difficulty thrusting up through this light gravel.

Serious enthusiasts wrap containers in bubble plastic and sensitive woody shrubs in sacking or pipe insulation. This, however, does detract from the pleasure of seeing the bare bones of the winter garden. I shall put my faith in inconspicuous surface mulches and hope that next spring the bones will not be dead.

1994

Acidantheras and Kaffir lilies

One is sometimes tempted to suspect that the free bonus plants offered as an inducement to mail-order purchasers are simply a method by which the nurseries disperse stock for which they have no ready market. This may be for one of two reasons: a failure to catch the public's attention, or because of the unsuitability of that plant for cultivation without specialist skills.

Some years ago I received such a freebie from Hortico—a dozen small corms of *Acidanthera bicolor murielae* (now also called *Gladiolus callianthus*), an Ethiopian member of the iris family, said to flower in sunny borders from August to October. Each year they put up a good head of leaves, almost indistinguishable from *Crocosmia*, and each year I lifted them on the advent of winter frosts without having seen a trace of a flower.

I learnt from sources less optimistic than the Hortico catalogue that August flowering was highly unlikely and that most success with acidantheras came to gardeners in the warmest and most southerly parts of Britain, or to those with sunny conservatories. This year, therefore, I changed my strategem, and planted the corms around the periphery of a large shallow pot containing three morning glory seedlings, and nestling against a warm west-facing wall.

At last it all seems worthwhile, and I must acknowledge that acidanthera is not so much a waste of time as a grossly underrated autumn flower. Graceful arching stems rear from each flat fan of leaves, supporting a skein of white butterfly flowers, each hovering on its long curving perianth tube.

The petal bases are marked with dark purple and the flower emits a powerful and exotic scent. Up to ten flowers open in succession upon the tall stems, the new buds projecting like darts above the open blooms.

Frost will, in due course, threaten these magical flowers, and then I shall as usual lift and store the corms. However, a sunny wall acts like a night storage heater on reverse timing, charging up in the sunshine and releasing its heat into the chilly night. With luck it will radiate sufficient heat to stave off November ground frosts until the flowers are spent.

A smaller and less demanding member of the Iridaceae or iris family is *Schizostylis coccinea*, the Kaffir lily of Southern Africa. This flowers reliably in late autumn in an ordinary border and grows from a tangled mass of fleshy rhizomes which need not be lifted in the winter. Spikes of bright glossy scarlet or dark pink flowers are borne on stems one and a half to two feet tall, while the early-flowering variety 'Mrs Hegarty' has exquisite clear pink blooms. Schizostylis makes an excellent cut flower, as evocative of autumn as freesias are of spring. If only it also boasted the heady fragrance of a freesia or an acidanthera, it would be perfect.

1990

Gardeners World comes to Carrog

When the BBC TV series *Gardeners World* asked to visit Carrog, to film the autumn colour for their 1992 new series, owners Geoffrey and Maureen Williams were warned that they might find the experience 'very invasive'.

Picturing giant grey BBC vans, miles of cable and the chance to see all sorts of exotic personnel like 'The Gaffer' and 'The Best Boy', I eagerly accepted Mrs Williams's invitation to go and observe. In complete contrast, the whole exercise involved just three cars, four people, and what seemed like miles of wandering Carrog's meandering paths and lawns in search of choicely lit shrubs, exquisite berries and one another.

The technical crew (who had just finished filming *Trainer* for the BBC) consisted of a cameraman and a sound man linked between their machines by a strong umbilicus of cable. They worked their way around the garden shooting shrubs and trees, berries and vistas. They carried a pair of secateurs with which to tidy up stray stems on otherwise faultless hydrangeas and on the staccato shout of 'sound', we all froze, the camera rolled, and a phlegmatic robin would promptly begin its routine.

More peripheral to proceedings were the film's presenter, *Daily Telegraph* gardening columnist Stephen Lacey and Maureen Williams, part owner and principal gardener of Carrog. Elegantly clad as far as the knees (gardener's wellies beneath), Mrs Williams had been led to expect an informal interview with Stephen Lacey, and to be asked difficult questions such as 'what was your objective in creating the garden?'

One wonders sometimes whether just liking plants has become an insufficient qualification for a media gardener.

During my five hours as an observer, this interview never took place since the producer was, quite rightly, reluctant to waste scant October sunshine on people when it could be employed so much more lustrously on plants. Instead a rambling debate among the bystanders revolved around where Mr Lacey and Mrs Williams should seat themselves for their discussion. Here Carrog proved sadly deficient: no seats, no rustic rocks, no convenient low boughs whatever. When

Geoffrey Williams sits in his garden it is on the ride-on mower. If Maureen Williams sits, it is on the grass.

A small stone bench by the back door was located and Stephen Lacey was eager to have it moved to a tranquil spot between three silver-barked birch trees for their spontaneous chat. It seemed likely, if inadvisable, that the film crew could carry it there. However, Carrog's five acres of autumnal finery continued to beckon the film crew and by late afternoon the seat remained unmoved, presenter and owner unused, and the light had faded from the yellowing birch leaves.

By this time the chief preoccupation was searching the garden for an *Acer palmatum dissectum* still warmed by the low afternoon sun. Perhaps a chainsaw could have cleared a light line, but each shaggy bush now lurked in the misty dim. The team agreed to return on the morrow.

1991

The ways of NAFAS ladies

Iona Trevor-Jones is an icon in the flower-arranging world. Nearly fifty years of her life have been devoted to her art, during which time she has collected innumerable awards and given countless demonstrations, travelling as guest expert and judge to far-flung corners of the world, and hosting floral events at her former home near Welshpool. Among her credits were the floral decorations for the Investiture of the Prince of Wales. The first president of NAFAS (The National Association of Flower Arrangement Societies) described her as the most prolific award winner of them all. Now over seventy, she still arranges and lectures indefatigably from her retirement home near Lampeter.

I on the other hand am a complete philistine: I delight in my flowers, and ram them joyfully into vases, but have never decorated a church in my life. It was therefore instructive to see a review copy of Mrs Trevor-Jones's newly released video, 'The Expert Flower Arranger', in which we see her strolling in her garden collecting her material, and creating a series of formal arrangements: a bridal display, pedestals to flank the altar in St Peter's Church, Lampeter, a 'Continental' display for a side-chapel altar and some bowls and arrangements for the home. As she arranges she talks, effortlessly, receiving flowers one by one from her barely visible assistant Jean, who seldom falters in providing the next appropriate bloom, already de-leafed and cut to length. NAFAS ladies demand high standards. 'There's been a little bug at that,' she says, handing a pink rose she called 'Felicity' back to the invisible Jean. 'A little leaf there,' mercilessly plucking the offending item from an imperfectly defoliated spray of stephanandra. I wondered absently at the unfamiliar look of the white lilies in the bridal display. Then it dawned: their golden wobbly stamens had been individually snipped out. 'Have to watch for a stamen there, Jean,' as an unruly bud threatened to unfurl under the camera lights. Jean will be there with the scissors, lest pollen soil the bride's dress.

Although flower arranging has developed its own vocabulary and codes of conduct to elevate it to the level of a science, it is a science in which old dogmas are rapidly replaced by new ones. Mrs Trevor-Jones reminisces upon the importance of the 'focal point' or 'centre of interest' in the days of Constance Spry. These terms have lost their importance, and flower arrangers now seem to defer to new pundits, with 'planes of leaves' and 'blocks of colour' dictated by the now fashionable 'continental' style in arranging. I personally took least pleasure in the 'Continental' church arrangement, in which flowers, foliage and a group of globe artichokes formed separate disciplined lines and blocks as if ranged for sale on a costermonger's stand.

I did enjoy the glimpses of Mrs Trevor-Jones's garden which the film allowed. Variegated foliage is a great boon to flower arranging, and here were gold and white-edged hostas, a variegated *Acer drummondii*, a magnificent variegated phlox, and that white-leaved poplar *Populus x candicans* 'Aurora'. It was useful to be reminded that this tree should be cut hard in February to produce new vigorous white-tipped shoots. I like it much better as a foil to flower arranging than as a large tree.

1994

Ornamental cabbages in Aberystwyth

Even on a wet and rainy day there are about a hundred heads clustered behind the seats at the top of Great Darkgate Street. They are attracting the attention of many passers-by, who pause and look again, for what at first glance appears to be a neat display of white and purple flowers is nothing of the sort. It is a bed of cabbages.

This bedding scheme, in the L-shaped bed which backs the small lawn opposite the Town Clock Square, is the brainchild of John Shipman, Ceredigion District Council Horticultural and Landscaping Officer. He is an exciting innovator in local civic gardening, bringing unusual and unfamiliar plants to the town planters, and subtle colour schemes to our flower beds. He came close, in 1989, to taking the Wales in Bloom Trophy for Aberystwyth, for the quality of the summer displays. His cabbages are a triumph, a crisp bright display, almost luminous on a grey day, and bringing a smile to many a weary shopper.

The plants are of an ornamental strain of cabbages, Tokyo Mixed F_1 hybrid, and were grown from seed at the council nurseries. Three different forms resulted in unpredictable proportions. Commonest are the green and purple variety, whose dull green outer leaves embrace a dense crown of puce-purple as brilliant as any flower. Interplanted with these are a green and white variety, laced and fringed with cream to give a frilly appearance to the plant. Least abundant is a pink and green form, in which pink is substituted for the cream.

Winter cabbages do not suffer the attack of caterpillars, so they should remain in pristine form until mid-April, when they will be removed to make way for spring bedding before bolting into flower.

Perhaps the greatest threat to the border is posed by humorous thieves with culinary intent. Setting aside the criminal nature of such an act, I am told that like many varieties of plants bred for their decorative qualities, as food Tokyo F_1 cabbages leave much to be desired. They are not a popular salad cabbage despite their prettiness, and are unduly chewy when cooked.

Next year John Shipman plans to add an ornamental kale, 'Peacock', to his range of winter foliage plants, and perhaps cabbages will move on to conquer more beds presently given over to polyanthus. Housholders could follow suit by replanting their summer window boxes with Tokyo cabbages. Their colours complement the local stone, and their robust form will resist the buffeting on even a seriously windy corner.

1990

The weird colour of the callicarpa

The first time I saw *Callicarpa bodinieri* I thought it was a hoax, so improbable is this graceful Chinese shrub. Lost in the shrub border for the rest of the year, it excels itself in the autumn with arching branches laden with regularly spaced clusters of atrociously vivid purple berries. The first thing that came to my mind was those gaudy plastic popper beads of which so many early sixties necklaces were made. The birds, like me, seem in two minds about callicarpa: although they do eat them it is as a last resort, and the bushes remain gaudily bejewelled long after more familiar pyracantha and cotoneaster have been stripped of every berry. The shrub is fully hardy and likes an acid soil. It would make a striking statement against a grey local stone cottage wall, perhaps in contrast with the piquant yellow blooms of winter jasmine.

Another magic berry is that of *Viburnum davidii*, a big bush with dark leathery well-marked oval leaves and umbels of tiny unexciting pinky white spring flowers. The pointed metallic-blue fruits are an autumn eye-catcher, and throughout the year the shrub makes a bold if sombre sculptural statement. I might plant it with some white-berried skimmias, *Skimmia japonica* 'Fructu Albo' for company. These shrubs look extraordinarily spruce all the year round and have neat evergreen leaves. Gleaming red-berried skimmias are a familiar sight around Aberystwyth (to the casual glance they could be dismissed as thornless hollies); the white variety deserves to be better known.

All these exciting shrubs have a single special requirement too easily overlooked by the casual visitor to the garden centre. Cross-pollination is often necessary for berry formation, and many berry-forming species actually have separate male and female plants. Thus a lone holly seldom berries, and where *Skimmia japonica* and *Viburnum davidii* are grown, separate male and female plants must be purchased. Callicarpa has both nurseryman of Bristol, in 1832, which can be seen in the National Library of Wales.

The setting of Nanteos seems caught in a time warp; Gary Hesp's commitment to it promises to prevent its destination being a black hole.

1994

The mechanisms of autumn colour

Grumbling about the autumn colour is an essential part of the British gardening temperament, an extension of our national tendency to comment unfavourably upon the weather. It comes as something of a surprise to find that in this autumn's display there are few grounds for complaint. Whole hillsides of native deciduous woodland glow orange and russet, the trees brilliantly autumnal yet fully clothed in leaves.

Sycamore and young elm trees contribute a clear yellow, oaks, beeches and birches a brilliant russet and larches a contrasting yellowy green. In hedgerows the autumn shades of gold enhance the scarlet sprays of rose hips and the purplish haze of dense masses of red hawthorn berries on black, leafless twigs. In the garden, too, many shrubs are doing themselves justice this year. My small dogwood, *Cornus kousa*, which last year passed from green to leaflessness without a pause, stands like a candelabra, festooned with elongate, drooping peachy leaves, brilliant against the sombre backdrop of a privet hedge.

Amelanchier lamarckii, or snowy mespilus, colours similarly like the sunbathed face of a peach, becoming quite red in direct sunlight, while *Fothergilla monticola* remains a clear cadmium yellow. This shrub is a joy in spring for its white bottle-brush flowers which open over a long period, before and after the emergence of the leaves. I have not always found it reliable for autumn colour.

The Japanese maples have been puzzlingly diverse in their autumn behaviour. *Acer palmatum* and its smaller variety *Acer palmatum* 'Osakazuki' are clothed in brilliant red, while another popular variety, *Acer palmatum dissectum,* has long shed its leaves. My *Acer japonicum* 'Aconitifolium', whose leaves should, in Japan, have turned a marvellous yellow marbled red at the margins, has done likewise and stands bare, its fat buds anticipating the spring.

For most, if not all, ornamental and native trees, this autumn has offered the correct combination of sunny days and cool but not too frosty nights. Yellowness in leaves we can rely upon, for this derives from the carotene and xanthophyll pigments present in the leaves throughout their lives. As autumn sets in, chlorophyll, the green pigment in the leaf, is no longer replaced and simply fades away, allowing the golden hues to show through. Too sharp a frost, however, will kill the leaves outright and ensure their prompt fall.

For stronger colours, sunshine is essential in conjunction with night coolness. In these conditions sugar is made in the leaf during the day but cannot be transported at night to storage sites in the stem and roots. Instead, new pigments are formed—flavones (orange), anthocyanins (red-purple), and ellagitannins (pinky red) in exotic trees like dogwoods, sumach and tupelo.

The beauty and variety of autumn colour is in many ways far more of a marvel and a mystery than the glory of flowers. The extraordinary colours and forms of flowers have at least developed for a purpose—if not to gladden our own eyes, then at least to entice those of insects. Some elaborate forms even deceive, such as the bee orchids, which are designed to be mistaken by one bee for another of its kind, or the blow-fly pollinated flowers which mimic rotten meat.

Autumn shades, by comparison, seem to serve no purpose, and are the purely accidental by-products of the deciduous tree 'shutting down production' for the winter.

1990

Carrog: the end of an era

My developing obsession as a gardener has been fuelled during my years in Wales by two very different examples set by expert practitioners of the craft. One has been the spectacle of those luxuriant bouquets, entitled 'Vase of flowers from Competitor's own Garden' which appear on the benches of the village shows. They inspired me to realize that my own garden could be harnessed to produce similar delights. The other great influence was Carrog.

We cannot all re-create Carrog in the confines of our own plot, but almost everyone used to visit it on the annual June open day in support of the National Gardens Scheme. It is a five-acre garden, sheltered from the salt-laden winds by the tree-clad ridge which conceals Llanddeiniol from view from the A487. Once there, the feeling was gentle and enfolding. The sweep of perfectly tended lawn drew the eye from the house towards luxuriant borders, brimming with shrub roses, strange and unfamiliar types of hydrangeas, vast blue-green hosta leaves and brilliant tree peonies. Lawned walks led one through a dizzy assortment of unfamiliar shrubs, down to the pond bordered by the ornamental leaves of the giant *Gunnera manicata*, by skunk cabbage and handsome bronze-leaved rodgersias. Returning towards the house one entered the walled kitchen garden, its perimeter a haven for diverse tender plants, and passed into the exquisite world of the orchid-filled conservatory.

This year marks the end of an era, with the deaths, in spring and in autumn respectively, of the garden's modest creators, Geoffrey and Maureen Williams. Motivated by a fascination for plants, Maureen was a discriminating collector, who purchased steadily from quality suppliers, and planted the present garden within the setting of mature native trees. Unaided, the couple maintained the garden entirely by their own labour. During the summer months Geoffrey Williams would complete a weekly tour of five hours ride-on lawn mowing, and control the weeds in the shrub borders by careful spray applications of Tumbleweed. Maureen's skilled use of companion planting and extensive impenetrable ground cover made this relatively low-maintenance gardening possible.

For twenty-two consecutive years the open day was a high point of the local calendar, where gardeners gazed wistfully at an inspirational collection, and others came as much to enjoy the garden party ambience, and the quality tea. Two years ago the Williamses received the award of a ceremonial trowel from the NGS organisers to mark this achievement.

Riding on the back of their public opening came media prominence, glowing entries in the *Good Gardens Guide, The Shell Guide to Gardens*, and appearances on BBC *Gardeners World*, S4C's *Ar Y Tir*, and Radio Cymru. Pundits came and tried to place Maureen in a mould, asking her to define her objectives in creating the garden, or quite incorrectly designating it a garden created for autumn colour alone. But Maureen was what one would recognize as a real gardener. She chose plants because she loved them and she planted them where they would thrive and please her eye. She leaves a garden which is not 'designed' but which developed, and which is a lasting statement of her love of plants.

1994

The celebrity speaker crosses the mountains

Every year the Cardiganshire Horticultural Society includes in its programme a 'Celebrity Lecture', a big name in the gardening world who must be lured, with substantial libations of dosh, to cross the border, negotiate the picturesque contortions of the A44, and appear, spruce and cheerful before the audience in the Botany Lecture Theatre on the Penglais campus at Aberystwyth.

By tradition, this exotic one-day-migrant arrives in October, softens up the audience with some highly complimentary remarks about the Welsh landscape and then launches into the talk which, being a Celebrity, he or she will have given many times before. Last year's visitor, Daphne Ledward, was informative but supremely irrelevant as she lectured her audience on the problems of gardening on East Anglian clay. Only those planning a profound easterly move needed to take many notes.

This year's speaker, Nigel Colborn, used the occasion to promote his book, *This Gardening Business*, published by Cassells at £9.95, which he ingenuously offered for sale at a round £10 having omitted to provide any change. The talk was a polished delivery, of the after-dinner speech variety, with lots of jokes and well marked pauses to invite and accommodate the laughs. Since he was speaking to the title 'Humour and Entertainment for Gardeners', no one could complain that they were misled in receiving a frivolous and anecdotal address. There were some pleasing tales about his experiences as a nurseryman, and in opening his garden to public gaze, and a delightful quotation from the diaries of Swedish plant collector Carl Thunberg (of, among other plants, *Berberis thunbergii* fame) whose description of his own heroism when floundering on horseback in a fast-flowing river would have done justice to Kenneth Grahame's Mr Toad.

Demanding, and receiving, a free copy of *This Gardening Business* for review purposes, I felt slightly guilty at depriving him of his tenner. However, having read the book, a light-hearted exposition of how to elevate oneself to the ranks of the gardening expert, I realize that I acted like a true professional. Here are detailed expositions of how to conceal one's ignorance of plant names through audacious untruthfulness, the rules of one-upmanship of Flower Shows, the pitfalls for nurseryman and garden owner, and most significantly, the low-down on how to lecture and to demand a huge fee. Strategems for ensuring that tight-fisted garden visitors pay their entrance fee and garden club treasurers part with the maximum they can afford plus VAT lose one's sympathy as the book reveals the relative affluence of the author.

A great many types of people are held up to ridicule in Mr Colborn's book: northerners, people without 'O' levels, people who cannot pronounce French wines correctly, fuchsia and pelargonium enthusiasts, lady dahlia growers, and perhaps most of all, those whose lack of a classical education prevents their instant comprehension of Latin names. A glossary devoted to misinformation abounds with joky definitions of species names such as *candidum* 'about to stand for Parliament' or *paniculata* 'suitable for frying'.

If, like the author, I owned a manor house with four WCs, I should keep this book in a remote one, where it would receive the casual attention it deserves.

1992

Quest for the perfect Christmas tree

An annual ritual in my family has long been the quest for the perfect Christmas tree. Visiting the local market of my Yorkshire childhood we would scrutinize dozens of trees, inspecting them from every angle for symmetry, bushiness and strong shapely upper twigs from which presents and baubles could freely hang. All seemed fresh and fragrant, but once brought into the warmth of the house the real test began. Some trees would promptly shed their needles in showers, till by Twelfth Night the upper twigs stood knobbly and brown, the carpet prickly and green. It was not unusual to find dry spiky needles readily dislodged by Christmas Day.

Only since moving to Wales have I discovered the joy of a really fresh-cut Christmas tree, its foliage pliant and feathery to the touch, still green and aromatic with resin when consigned to the January bonfire. Yet despite the substantial amount of Christmas tree production in our area, shop-bought trees cannot be relied upon. I learnt from a Forestry Commission forester that trees are generally cut by mid-November, partly to ensure that December snow on high ground does not impede the harvest. Many are also just tops from larger trees, a by-product of timber production. Cut up to six weeks before Christmas, the shock of a warm house can be disastrous.

Instead we make an idyllic visit to David Hides's small plantation at Hengwm, Llangorwen, and select our tree on the root. Hengwm, a lone cottage approached by a side turning shortly below the hairpin bend at Cwmcynfelin, comes with an acre of land behind the house, steeply sloping, north-facing and deep in winter shade. Last December, after several days of blue winter cold the hillside was rimed in a deep growth of hoar-frost, each night's crystals layered on the last until it looked and felt like a dusting of snow. The village of Llangorwen below basked frost-free in the winter sunshine.

Not finding it an easy situation for an extensive garden, David Hides, who is a grass expert at the Welsh Plant Breeding Station, planted Christmas trees, *Picea abies*, and enters into the spirit of the trade with all the enthusiasm of the hobbyist grower.

A small selection of freshly cut trees are always ready to take away, but keen family parties troop up the hillside with David and the bow saw to make the ultimate in personal choice. Each tree seemed slightly better than the last, until we settled upon one embellished with an old thrushes' nest in the lower branches which we prized as much as any gaudy decoration.

David Hides buys in young trees and replants the gaps in his plantation with eighteen-inch saplings in March of each year. (He does not grow the noble fir, *Abies procera,* which has also become popular for its stiffer bluish foliage in recent years. This is a slower growing and much more expensive tree.) For two years the newly planted Christmas trees consolidate their position but increase little in size. Thereafter growth is rapid and a three-foot tree (the height to the top whorl of twigs, not the central spike) takes just five years from planting. A good floor-to-ceiling tree eight or nine feet tall takes only three years more.

Whisked straight from the plantation to the house, fresh trees are very thirsty and a proprietory tree-stand with a deep reservoir of water is well worth having. Thus regularly watered and refreshed it is barely messier than an artifical tree.

1991

Sexing the holly

The holly is a shrub, or indeed, given time, a substantial tree, which we tend to take for granted as a provider of Christmas berries but overlook when planting a garden. Prompted by its reputation as a slow grower, many gardeners accept a holly gratefully if it comes with the garden, but too few plant hollies in the situations the tree deserves.

As a specimen tree more hedgerows deserve an unrestrained common holly, *Ilex aquifolium*, the traditional spiny, dark green Christmas holly, adorned, if in good company, with a crop of bright gleaming red berries, each standing on its own little stem. Hollies can attain a height of seventy feet, and form a pleasing loosely pyramidal tree. Too often they start out as opportunistic seedlings and their shape is distorted by the company in which they grew. A good cultivar is the yellow-berried variety, *Ilex aquifolium bacciflava*, which is sometimes to be found in the front gardens of substantial Victorian houses. Almost thornless hollies with extra-large gleaming red fruits are likely to be cultivars of Highclere holly, *Ilex* x *altaclerensis*, a hybrid between our common holly and the Canary holly, *Ilex perado*, which arose in the gardens of Highclere Castle near Newbury.

Fruiting is, however, dependent upon the availability of a mate, for hollies are single-sexed trees, and the female plants develop berries only if they have been pollinated by a male. If you have a sulky holly of unknown variety failing to justify itself in the garden, it will soon be time to establish whether the problem is that it is male, or that it is lonely. Look closely where next year's berries ought to be, around the twig not far from the tip of the shoot, and already small, tight dull white buds are detectable. In February or March these tiny flowers will open, four petals, four stamens spreading from a central boss. Look closely here, for a female plant has at the flower centre a raised green four-lobed crown, topped off with the flat disc of the stigma. Here is berry potential, provided a male is planted nearby. Male flowers by contrast have larger stamens arising from a recessed centre.

For hedging, or for topiary purposes, a male holly may well be preferable to a female. Spring pruning will, after all, severely curtail berries on a neatly trimmed plant, so foliage character is more important. To repel the most intrusive visitors I would plant *Ilex aquifolium* 'Ferox', a small-leaved intensely prickly male holly, which will make an impenetrable barrier. Just be sure to wear gardening gloves when clearing up fallen leaves from the border. Less ferocious, and more colourful, is the gold-edged male holly *Ilex aquifolium* 'Argentea Marginata', or the almost spineless *Ilex* x *altaclerensis* 'Golden King'. This last is in fact a female but fruits so sparingly one would scarcely notice.

In selecting an appropriate sex of holly, it is vital to abandon all common sense when considering the named varieties, and to depend on a good book or a reliable nurseryman. 'Golden Queen' and 'Silver Queen' are in fact male, regal only for their foliage variagation, while against the odds, 'Golden King' is a female. It comes as a welcome relief to find that 'Golden Milkboy' at least is masculine.

Making an appearance at the garden centres is another holly species, *Ilex* x *meserveae*, with cultivars 'Blue Princess' and 'Blue Angel'.